SIMON AND

SCHUSTER

NEW YORK

LONDON

TORONTO

SYDNEY

TOKYO

Lifespring

GETTING

YOURSELF

FROM

WHERE

YOU ARE

TO WHERE

YOU WANT

TO BE

JOHN HANLEY

Simon and Schuster
Simon & Schuster Building
Rockefeller Center
1230 Avenue of the Americas
New York, New York 10020

SIMON AND SCHUSTER and colophon are registered trademarks of
Simon & Schuster Inc.

DESIGNED BY BARBARA MARKS GRAPHIC DESIGN/LYNNE KOPCIK
Manufactured in the United States of America

10   9   8   7   6   5   4   3   2   1

Library of Congress Cataloging in Publication Data
Hanley, John.
  Lifespring: getting yourself from where you are to where you want
to be/John Hanley.
      p.   cm.
    1. Conduct of life.   I. Title.
BJ1581.2.H255   1989
158'.1—dc19   89-4136
                                                                   CIP

ISBN 0-671-64643-5

This book is dedicated to Candace, my wife, my partner in the dance of life for the last twenty-four years. She is committed to my showing up as a possibility.

ACKNOWLEDGMENTS

A special acknowledgment and my deep appreciation to Liz Swerling, the project director for this book. Without Liz's collaboration there would be no book.

To Denny McGinnis, my unparalleled assistant who makes a difference in my work daily, my love and thanks.

My gratitude goes to the following people for their contributions to this book. From generating ideas, to research, to editing, these individuals have been champions of this project: Corbin Collins, Ph.D., Hubert Dreyfus, Ph.D., John Enright, Ph.D., Ellie Hanauer, Stuart Gelles, John Hanley, Jr., Laurie Lister, Robert Slagle, Ph.D., and the Lifespring trainer body.

My special thanks to those people who agreed to be interviewed, to open up their private thoughts and feelings, and to go public with what happened for them during and after their Lifespring trainings: Gerry Beemiller, Gene Ciancio, Drucie French-Cumbie, Bill Garrett, Lisa Hoffman-Ciancio, Jim Kelly, Rosalie Maretsky, Charlie Morf, Linda Rosso, Helen Shreves, Debbie Stamper, Greg Walker, Skip Williams, Dave Zoller and Joan Zoller.

Finally, and perhaps most importantly, my sincere appreciation and respect to the people who, for the last fifteen years, have made my life worth getting out of bed in the morning: Lifespring graduates nationwide.

CONTENTS

CONTENTS

Introduction

As adults in our society, we are presumed to be competent and productive in many arenas: for example, love, career, relationships and family, personal responsibility, communication, making and keeping commitments. But where and when were we supposed to learn about and get coached in these subjects?

Ironically, traditional educational methods do not teach us to be proficient in many of the arenas that are the greatest sources of satisfaction, joy, and accomplishment in adult life. It turns out that learning about the issues that fundamentally define adulthood has been, for all of us, pretty much a sink or swim proposition. With no formal curriculum to help, we have had to learn the hard way, on our own, through the school of hard knocks.

The Lifespring educational methodology is a breakthrough in adult education. It provides a scientifically validated structure for you to get behind the everyday business of living, dedicate yourself to your deepest commitments, and act more effectively in the areas of your life that matter most to you.

Lifespring is an organization dedicated to furthering the highest aspirations of each and every human being. We are committed to serving people in a special way that enhances personal dignity, responsibility, accomplishment, and freedom. Lifespring is for people who are committed to accomplishing extraordinary results while celebrating the profound privilege and exhilaration of being alive.

I promise that as a result of your sincere participation with Lifespring, whether through training sessions or this book, you will discover a new spectrum of possibilities for your personal fulfillment and accomplishment. Lifespring gives you an opportunity to shift your ability to think and act effectively in the face of a wider range of challenges.

Your personal goal may be to enhance specific skills or abilities, or to further explore that unnameable mystery of the human experience which is essential and sublime. No matter what your motivation or particular concerns are, you can count on your involvement with Lifespring to support you in taking actions that enhance the quality of your life in important and meaningful ways.

THE LIFESPRING BASIC TRAINING

This book contains a majority of the content of the Lifespring Basic Training. Of course, the actual training, which consists of groups of 150–250 people interacting together with a common purpose, is impossible to recreate with ink on paper. To have the kind of breakthrough that happens for people in the Basic requires doing the Basic; there is no replacement. However, this book presents the same material in a way that you can have access to breakthrough in your own life whether or not you participate in the Basic Training.

Explaining the training is a problem given that it is either unlike anything else you have ever experienced, in which case you will have difficulty relating to what I say about it, or similar to something else you have experienced, in which case you are likely to make incorrect assumptions about it. The value in reading this book, as in the Basic Training—and in life—depends on your full participation and your willingness to experience something unpredictable.

NONTRADITIONAL EDUCATION

What does Lifespring's nontraditional educational methodology accomplish that traditional educational models don't?

The issues that determine the quality of adult life are not fully accessible intellectually; they also need to be experienced. Lifespring's method of education is *experiential*. Our curriculum addresses issues that require experience to be understood. These are issues that all adults face: communication, giving and receiving feedback, honesty, commitment, dignity, knowing what is important to you and acting on it effectively, personal responsibility, living with vitality and passion. Rather than getting information through lectures, being force-fed facts and figures, you participate in the learning process; you are teacher and student, observer and observed. Rather than the "school of hard knocks," you can explore those issues in a safe and supportive learning environment by participating in games and exercises that are metaphors for life and, therefore, experiential in nature. For instance, rather than being told about the concept of honesty, you are put in a situation that allows you either to be honest or not, to examine your behavior and to experience directly the effect your behavior has on others by observing their reactions and getting their feedback. From that experience, you can learn something about honesty in other areas of your life. Observing yourself in action can bring to the foreground beliefs and behaviors that you don't normally notice, but that absolutely influence your effectiveness and satisfaction.

In the context of traditional learning, if you engage in assertiveness training, you can expect to come out with tools to assist you in being more assertive and confident; if you take a time-management course, you will be told how to better manage your time; if you take cooking lessons, you will get information about being a more proficient cook. These are the promised results of traditional educational models: to give you information and/or teach you to manipulate your behavior so as to have life be "more, better, different." However, if traditional education were 100 percent effective itself, why then would you *ever* take another class in time management or read another book about better relationships? Didn't you learn it already? Why would you still be struggling with the things in life that you are struggling with—didn't they have books and classes about those things when you were in school? The thing is, life rarely occurs the way books or lectures tell you it does.

There are countless examples of situations in life that are completely unlike how you were taught they would be. Take your first date or your first kiss, for example. Were they anything like what you were led to believe they would be? An example from my own life that demonstrates how different real life is from how they teach you it's going to be was the birth of my daughter. She is our third child, and was born at a time when natural childbirth was an available option. My wife and I took our Lamaze classes every week and we were excellent students—we knew everything there was to know for a smooth, loving, fulfilling birth. Then she went into labor. No problem—off to the hospital we went. To any of you who have experienced the birth of a baby, I don't need to tell you how different it was from anything we had been taught. One of my more sentimental recollections is of the moment when my wife screamed, "Get me drugs, now!" The classes were informative and helpful, but we could not have anticipated or mastered the demands of the real life event until we were in it. It's like the difference between reading a book on biking and getting on a bike. If all you've done is read the book, the first time out on the bike is going to be a struggle. But, once you've actually ridden, you will always have that experience to draw upon. It literally becomes part of you. Likewise, once you have struggled with the personal lessons you need to learn, you will be equipped with the experience and the practices that can maximize your effectiveness and personal fulfillment in *all* circumstances, in *all* areas of your life, *forever*.

Lifespring and traditional education can complement each other in practical ways. The Lifespring methodology is designed as a vehicle not for improving on the rational, information-based structure of traditional education, but for pioneering within that tradition. A broad and balanced educational menu will best support you in breakthrough.

Richard Linowes, a professor of business at the American University in Washington, DC, remarks that, "One of the things I really was fascinated by in the course is that it's a different methodology for teaching. It's different from anything that I have experienced, even in some very fine schools. I would say that this weekend course was better than any course I took in any university I ever attended, including several years at Harvard Business School. As an educator, I look forward to this being part of mainstream education as soon as universities are prepared to offer it. I think this kind of training should be offered by the YMCA, by church groups, by universities—right now, it's offered by a company called Lifespring."

INQUIRY AND NEW POSSIBILITIES

The most relentless enemy to learning is what you already know. This is a pretty radical statement. For most of us, schooling focused on information, logic, and answers as the cornerstones of learning. Virtually every investigation or inquiry was undertaken to arrive at a concrete conclusion, and to expand our reservoirs of factual knowledge. Accuracy and style of presentation were the keys to success. In contrast, the Lifespring trainings open another avenue for learning. They are inquiries which provide opportunities to explore what is invisible in most educational settings: how you think; why you see the world the way you do; what your predetermined assumptions about life are; and how your interpretations determine your identity, your behavior, and your accomplishments. We don't offer you answers or techniques, give you assignments, or test you on your recall. We engage you in a uniquely thought-provoking and stimulating journey into new territory.

The work we do at Lifespring is not about what you know, being right about what you know, acquiring more knowledge, providing answers, or acquiring on-the-job skills; it's not about filling in the blanks of what you know you don't know. This work is about uncovering *new possibilities*—expanding the opportunities available to you by allowing you to think and act in innovative ways. This work is about *what you don't know you don't know.*

"Possible" means being within the limits of ability, capacity, or realization; what may be done or may occur according to nature, custom, or manners; something that may or may not occur. Possibility, then, isn't some cosmic fantasy, hope, or wish.

It takes the conditions of a specific time and place in history to open up new possibilities. Space travel is a good example. Would flying to the moon have been possible for prehistoric human beings? No. Given their interpretation of the world, the possibility of space travel was not yet opened. Obviously the technology was not available, but more importantly, prehistoric human beings had no vision of or concern for getting to the moon. As we define it, possibility is grounded in temporal reality.

Possibilities are distinct from options; a possibility is something that doesn't exist, but could be invented, while options already exist. Lifespring's effectiveness is based on our ability to open up new possibilities through inquiry and invention rather than merely proposing answers or presenting finite options.

Although, by definition, what is possible is bound by the limits of what already is, we are less likely to be available to possibilities if we are searching for specific, absolute answers. There are no obvious or absolute answers to the complex questions of life. The conversation that engages you in questioning is one that allows for possibility and creativity. Inquiry for the sake of contemplation, however, is not the destination of our journey; it is merely the vehicle that will help transport us. Contemplation alone does not generate action. *You must harness your insights and consciously apply them to your practices in order to manifest what you say you want.*

ABOUT THIS BOOK

Like anything in life, the value for you in this process will depend on your participation. *There Is No Such Thing As A Free Lunch.* If you want results, it will take your own blood, sweat, and tears. You are smart to seek out the proven technology and expertise that can guide you and accelerate your progress; but always be aware that, in the end, the responsibility for your accomplishment is yours alone.

The great gods of excellence, accomplishment, and fulfillment don't care if you have a conceptual grasp of some good ideas and profound insights. Concepts and insights can be valuable steps in the process of transformation, but they are not sources of action, and alone they will not beget the rich harvest that our work is designed to generate. Excellence and fulfillment will come to you when you participate at a new level, and then require yourself to press out again to the next level.

So, what does "to participate at a new level" mean? For one thing, you will have to discipline yourself to quiet your opinions and judgments, and really *listen,* opening yourself to the possibility that there is always something new to learn. This does not mean that you must agree, understand, or approve, but merely that you be open enough to admit that you may not have all the answers, question your own assumptions, and be willing to entertain other points of view. Listen and consider with an open mind the ideas and questions posed here. But don't stop with this book. Listen and receive newly every person and every event in your life. So often we automatically approach situations combatively in order to protect our interests, demonstrate our superiority, or avoid feeling dominated. Instead, train yourself for a new approach. Enter every conversation or situation with these thoughts: "I wonder what this person/situation can teach me"; "I wonder whether considering this point of view could make a difference in my life"; "It would actually be exciting if I were wrong about X, Y, or Z!" Thus, one way of participating at a "new level" is to operate as though your experiences actually were new. Pretend that you are a beginner at life, anxious to gain from everyone else's experience. God gave you two ears and one mouth for a reason.

To give you an opportunity to listen for miracles, every other chapter of this book is the real-life story of a Lifespring graduate. These graduates represent the 300,000 who have completed the Lifespring Basic Training. Although those included in these pages tend to be high-powered professionals, one of the beauties of the Basic Training is that you will find people from very different social backgrounds echoing the very same themes about what it is to be a human being. The stories told here and the experiences of Lifespring graduates from all walks of life illustrate that, in the midst of all the abstract philosophy, the benefit of transformational work consists of the simple miracles that happen in people's lives as a result.

There are tangible ways you can assist yourself to operate at a new level. For example, devise ways to keep yourself conscious of the process throughout the day. Place notes in strategic places in your home, office, car, wallet. Choose a certain word each day that will remind you of your commitment every time you hear or speak it. Change something about your morning routine so that at the beginning of every day your automatic patterns are gently interrupted. Experiment with how you interact with people. For instance, if you notice you are avoiding someone, go talk to that person; if you usually only talk business with someone, ask about his or her family or recreational activities. The purpose of these experiments isn't to make any particular point, but merely to allow for new possibilities in your relationships with people, possibilities that may be blocked by routines into which you automatically fall.

Finally, I recommend you keep a journal. Throughout this book there are lists of questions to guide your personal inquiry. *Answer them* —they will be the most valuable part of this process if you are disciplined enough to use them to prompt your thinking. Take the time to answer them thoughtfully, and write your responses in the journal. Also, use your journal for recording spontaneous thoughts. Don't labor over what you are writing or how to write it. Just sit down and let it flow freely. It doesn't matter if you never read it again. The process of writing is a potent tool for revealing and focusing deep thought processes and experiences.

Most importantly, to maximize the value of this process, share yourself, your life, and what you are learning with others. The single most powerful tool for creation is conversation. Allow people to see aspects of you that you haven't previously made available. People are dying to be related to openly, authentically, straightforwardly, vulnerably. Take the initiative. It will contribute to them as well as to you.

Congratulations on demonstrating your commitment to life. Whatever your reasons for picking up this book, you have an opportunity to earn great rewards. I say "earn" great rewards because this is not the lazy person's guide to enlightenment. There are prices to pay and work to be done. There is no easy way to transform your life. The path may be simple, but it isn't easy.

MY COMMITMENT

I am committed to your producing extraordinary and tangible results in all areas of your life. I am committed to your developing your relationship with yourself so you can count on yourself in a new and meaningful way. The goal of this process is for you to have a new sense of mattering, so that you participate in your daily life in a way that produces unrivaled satisfaction, aliveness, and accomplishment.

Consider the following scenario as a metaphor for my purpose. There is a guy, Jimmy, whose mother calls up to him one morning in order to get him off to school on time. Jimmy doesn't answer. He pulls the covers over his head, hoping that she will forget about him. Minutes later, Jimmy's mom calls up to him again. His breakfast is getting cold. Jimmy debates whether it might not be beneficial to develop a sore throat about now. Finally, Jimmy's mom runs up the stairs, into Jimmy's room, and sits down on the bed next to him. She shakes him gently. He yawns and stretches, pretending to still be asleep. Jimmy's mom tells him to get out of bed and hurry up and get ready for school. Jimmy looks up at her and desperately pleads with her to let him stay home. He claims he can't take another day there—the teachers don't like him and the kids tease him. Jimmy's mom insists that he go to school. "Why?" he retorts. She responds with two reasons: "One, you're 40 years old. And two, you're the principal."

Similarly, the technology presented here is a wake-up call. It's about getting out of bed and seeing the world somewhat differently than you have been seeing it up to this point. While the above story is facetious, it is entirely possible for you to be functioning and yet be essentially asleep to what's possible in some areas of your life. Just as for Jimmy, there may be a price to pay for "getting out of bed" and facing your life with commitment and passion. But by getting up, you make available an array of possibilities that wouldn't otherwise exist for you. Furthermore, in areas where you consider yourself to be effective already, a new vision for your future could lead to even greater success.

I am dedicated to your effectively transcending the level at which you now operate. Since you are the player, winning the game of excellence is up to you and no one else. You must assume total ownership of this project. You must decide that the rewards are greater than the prices you might pay. You must be clear and specific regarding the potential future value so that you will continue in the face of inevitable breakdowns and setbacks. Finally, you must be willing to question yourself—willing to put aside your own system of interpretation and subordinate your own already existing beliefs for the sake of the inquiry.

Human beings are social beings by nature and, therefore, exist in relation to each other. Whether directly or indirectly, our interactions with each other are the source of empowerment and worthwhile accomplishment. I stand for your accomplishing what matters to you.

CAVEAT

A word of qualification: My approach here is very black-and-white. Life, however, is full of gray. I caution you against taking what is written here and accepting it as "The Truth," or trying to make a formula out of it. It won't work in real life when you are faced with the "maybes."

On the other hand, I encourage you to go all the way in exploring and examining the questions and ideas presented here. Try arguing the opposite point of view when you disagree with or don't understand something. Out of that exercise, you will create new possibilities for yourself.

Lifespring is not interested in telling you what to think, but, rather, in allowing you to see for yourself what your thinking is. This opportunity to see and reinterpret what was previously transparent to you provides new choices and new freedom for effective action in all aspects of living. What I *never* request is an unquestioning acceptance of dogmatic philosophy. Quite the opposite. I am requesting that you question everything I say, and more importantly, everything *you* say.

Greg Walker

GRADUATE PROFILE

Sometimes it takes a day or two for a participant to jump into the training process. Not so for Greg Walker, a 34-year-old angiographer for Harvard Medical School and attending physician at Massachusetts General Hospital. He began the process of discovery and rigorous self-examination from the very beginning of the Basic Training. "As the time for the training approached, I had this sense of anticipation. I had high expectations that the training was really going to be something big. As a result of those feelings, I was a little bit afraid. I kept thinking that if I really wanted to get out of it, I could say I'm on call. I realized that as often as thoughts of avoid-

21

ance were coming up, those were the very reasons why I should go ahead and do the training. My inclination to avoid only reinforced that I needed to come face-to-face with what I was trying to avoid.

"The first night we went through a long tedium about the ground rules that everyone would agree to during the training. To me, they were very straightforward, very easy to comprehend. However, to some other people in the group, they were absolutely a source of contention and every one of them had to be examined in minute detail. What I thought was easily a ten-minute process turned into a three-hour process, just to go over eight or nine rules.

"Then, after the rules were completed, we did an exercise where we wandered around the room and talked about trust. The thing that hit me right in the face was that two people came up to me and just flat out said 'I don't trust you.' I was really upset by that. On the way home (I was riding with a friend of mine who was also in the training, and who had been the person that originally introduced me to Lifespring) I was just screaming at my friend. 'How could you ever get me involved in something like this? I hate the trainer. He is a jerk. I cannot believe I've wasted this money, etc., etc.' My friend just suggested to me that something must have touched a real nerve for me that night, or I would not be reacting that way. He pointed out that all we had done that night was go over some rules, and do one exercise. He told me that if I walked away from it without finding out why I had that reaction, I'd be selling myself short.

"The next night started with people sharing. One of the people who had said he didn't trust me stood up. He shared that one of the revelations he had the night before was that through his whole life he had basically never trusted anybody. He found it very difficult to rely on other people; he tried to be totally self-sufficient in everything he did. He looked out for himself only and not for other people and, therefore, didn't allow anybody else to look out for him. While he was sharing, I remembered how angry I had been the night before—in large part because this same man had said he didn't trust me. It came to me in this flash that I had been making all this stuff up about his not trusting me. I was making it all *my* problem, like I was this totally untrustworthy person. I never even could see another possibility that this could be his problem; that he could have an issue with trust. He was probably walking around the room telling *everyone* that he did not trust them. Instead, I was so focused on me, me, me, that I could only interpret it as being an indictment of me. That experience showed me how narrow I can be in my vision of things. I saw that there are really huge possibilities that I could broaden myself and my perspective through interacting with other people, sharing their experiences, and listening to them elaborate on their lives."

Why did Greg do the Basic Training? "I guess I was looking for something without even knowing I was looking. I just had this constantly uneasy feeling about things. I was really successful in my career and my job is an exciting one. A lot of people dream of doing the kind of work I do. And yet, I just wasn't that excited about all of that. In terms of relationships, I only had a very limited number of friends, which I said was because I didn't take the time outside of my work to go out and meet other people. I knew, though, that that was only an excuse. I wasn't really extending myself to people.

"I heard about the Lifespring training from a friend of mine whom I hadn't seen in two or three years because he had moved away from Boston. We had had a major falling out before he left. When I bumped into him last summer, I noticed something really different about him. When I mentioned it to him, he started telling me about the Lifespring trainings, which he had done since we had last seen each other. Hearing him recount what had happened for him, and being able to see that there was an obvious difference in him interested me. I went to a Guest Event and was very impressed with the speaker and with what she said was possible in the training, so I registered.

"Another key experience for me during the training was an exercise in which I realized that all my life I had been living for what other people thought of me and not for myself. I was absolutely willing to be the person I thought I should be for my friends, my family, people I worked with, and the average man on the street, instead of the person I was. I was willing to have unbelievable inner feelings of turmoil. I was willing to live a life that was not full of happiness and joy, but was full of compromise. I realized in an instant that the key to a successful, happy, gratifying, effective life is not to live something I am not, or to try to be something that I can never be because in my heart it isn't really me.

"Once I had discovered that, I wanted to examine it further. I had learned something, but could I realistically live my life that way and put it into practice? In a small group exercise I started to look at this question more closely. I looked at how I had been letting my circumstances completely control me, rather than me controlling my circumstances. Although on paper I looked like a success, I had this feeling that if people really knew who I was, they would see that my life was just a mockery. I thought that if they knew the real me, that they really wouldn't like me, that they would reject who I really am. So I had put up this elaborate screen and my life was all about projecting this image of being a successful doctor. I only had a few friends with whom I'd allow myself to be absolutely who I am and really show when I was hurt, when I cried, or when I was terrified. Although I am a pretty emotional person, I always put up this big facade. I was just so afraid to really let people know who I was for fear I would be ridiculed or humiliated or made fun of.

"Just sharing this with my small group was stepping right into that fear. Instead of reacting the way I feared they would, I saw people in my group with tears in their eyes. I realized that I was really putting limitations on other people, assuming that they were not big enough to accept me just the way I am. So the training for me was all about self-acceptance, about taking delight in myself and the wonderful things about me. At the same time it was about accepting that there are things about me that aren't so great, but not letting those control me, handicap me, or run my life.

"I find that my life is so enriched by grasping a couple of very very simple concepts. That is something else I learned, that it helps not to make things so complicated. In the training there is this very simple approach to life that consists of just looking at things as they really are instead of trying to dream up some unbelievably complicated, convoluted, elaborate scheme for everything. Just being authentic is what really makes my life interesting. And it's what makes me the kind of person that people want to know, because they really get to see who I am and what makes me tick.

"Honesty was another big part of the training for me. By that I mean being honest with myself about what I stand for and being honest with other people. I had never before thought that I was dishonest. But, really, I was often telling people things that I thought they wanted to hear rather than what was really true for me. I realized in the training that I was really not serving people well by doing that —they really are counting on me to tell them the truth. Here's an example that coincidentally happened on Friday during the training while I was at work: One of the nice things about being at this famous hospital is that there are a lot of people who want you to come and work for them. Before the training, I was asked by a doctor in New

Mexico to come out and become the chief of one of the sections in his department. That is very, very flattering. I thought about it for a month and had pretty much decided, for an array of reasons, not to go. But when the doctor called me I told him I hadn't decided. He said he would give me another month to think it over. Then, a month later, on Friday of the Basic Training, I got a call from this doctor. I already knew 100 percent that there was no way I was going to take this offer. But I told him what I thought he wanted to hear. I ran the same story all over again about how honored I was, and how I was really trying to decide, and how I loved Boston, but I knew I wasn't going to be in New England for the rest of my life. And on and on and on. He said that he really needed to know by the following month and we hung up. After I hung up I realized that I had just done what I always did. I had been totally dishonest. And I hadn't helped out this doctor at all—all he wanted was a straight answer, yes or no, so he could start the ball rolling if I were going, or get another doctor to fill the position if I weren't. He wasn't going to think any less of me if I said no. So I picked up the phone and called him right back. I told him that I wanted to be totally honest with him, that the fact was I really had made up my mind, and that I was declining his invitation. He then told me how much he respected me for calling him back and telling him that, and he thanked me for handling it promptly so he could get on with things. After I hung up, I laughed because I'd had this turmoil for months about how to tell this guy that I was not going to accept his offer, and it had been so easy. I felt great about it and he felt great about it.

"Outside of my professional life, the training has also made a difference in my personal relationships. For instance, with my sister. She and I grew up very close, but yet constantly bickering with one another. In recent years, we would see each other about once a year. And initially in those meetings, it would be like we were strangers. We would say the words 'I love you,' but they were just words, the necessary thing to say. I don't think there was really the meaning behind them. After I did the training, I was able to open up more, tell her more about myself, things that I had never shared with her before, things that I had thought she might use as ammunition against me. Now I cannot imagine myself thinking that. At one point I shared some things with her that were very important to me that I had wanted to get off my chest. She grabbed my hands, looked into my eyes and told me how much she loved me and that there is nothing I could say or do that would make her love me less or not want to have me in her life. Now I find that everything I experience I want to let her know. Instead of trying to harbor those things, I want to share them. And the same is true with other people in my life.

"In another instance, I can still remember the day I was with a friend at the Marketplace. I was really upset about something and I got very emotional and the tears just started pouring. My friend couldn't believe that I was standing there in that crowded place with hundreds of people walking by, crying like a baby, but what was going on with us was more important to me than what anybody on the street thinks. I guarantee you that what the person on the street thinks ran my life for a long time. I'd been more concerned about what my friends would think about my sister than what she was going through—the person I've grown up with and lived with and loved all my life. How I looked to others, even strangers on the street, was more important than being authentic with the people I cared for. My concern for how I appeared controlled my life instead of being true to what really mattered to me. I was more concerned with appearances than substance. What's true for me now is that when my life is over and I'm gone from this earth, what I want to have ascribed to me is that I really cared about other people honestly and openly, not that I always looked slick and never embarrassed myself.

"In retrospect I can see how some of the exercises in the trainings are designed to provoke people to be themselves in the most pure, basic, simple ways. I feel like I was able to really let people see every bit of me. Even when I thought I looked ridiculous, I still felt a simple, human dignity at the core of my being.

"I don't think I can ever really be afraid of people again. Fear of rejection, humiliation, ridicule, the feeling that I'm not enough, often controlled me before. Now, those fears don't influence me much because I had an experience in the training of putting myself out on the line and having the results be far greater than I had ever hoped they would be. Not only didn't my fears come true, but people were really moved by my contribution.

"When I say that I believe in the trainings, what I mean is I believe in people stopping and critically examining their lives and then getting a handle on what, in fact, their lives *could* be. And then, with that vision and knowledge, acting on that possibility. In the trainings we talk about an opening or an interruption, something that gets us to just stop, take a look, and realize, like I realized in that exercise on trust, that there are other possibilities for being that we have not even considered.''

This Book Is About Your Life

RESULTS

Hundreds of thousands of Lifespring graduates have turned possibilities into results. For instance, a New Jersey real estate broker reported that her yearly income jumped from $30,000 to $85,000 in the year following her Basic Training. She comments that "During the year following the Basic Training I realized that I was automatically using the principles that I had learned in the training when dealing with my clients. As a result of that my income almost tripled." She further reports that "I lost ten pounds. Also I became a very calm person. I now look at each problem as a challenge and instead of feeling despair I accept each challenge, solve the problem, and have a tremendous sense of achievement."

A Connecticut ophthalmologist informs us that "I totally changed my attitude toward my staff members. We are now partners in a common goal instead of adversaries. I make sure they win and thus I win." On a personal note, the same doctor shares that "My sons were barely speaking to me before I took the Basic Training. Now they call frequently, come home often, and are interested in what I am doing."

An engineering manager for TRW in Los Angeles calls the Basic Training "a supportive environment to look inside yourself for the answers to how you can be more effective, and live a richer, more fulfilling life." His own marriage "has become more open and intimate."

"I have actively participated in the peace movement since the early '60s," says a New Jersey psychologist. "Through Lifespring I have experienced an *internal* peace that had been missing." Her experience is echoed by a couple in New York. He, an international financier and attorney, says that "I have a great personal, inner peace." She, a professional artist: "I am 'at home' with myself for the first time in 37 years." As you can see, the benefits of participating with Lifespring range from measurable dollars and cents, to the elusive, priceless sense of having "come home" to yourself.

TAKING ACTION

I acknowledge you for seeking out this vehicle to forward yourself and I invite you to participate in this project as though your life depended on it. Be involved to such an extent that your behavior is "taken over" by your commitment to responsible and effective action. Allow for the possibility that your identity may be defined or redefined in some way through your participation. This is a big request. You can expect to question some of your primary beliefs and confront your automatic behaviors during this investigation. You may see that your beliefs—what you hold to be true about the world—are interpretations that don't serve you. You may likewise discover that some of your actions are counterproductive.

The people who are willing to pay the price now for long-term rewards are the ones who most dramatically transform their lives out of a project like this one. For them, the risks of inconvenience, embarrassment, failure, and other costs are worth the possible gains. The bottom line is "Pay the price now; or pay it later in life, with penalties and interest." The key is your willingness to change your practices, even in spite of not knowing for sure what the "right" practices are. It is certain that neither you nor any other human being can tap into new possibilities by sticking with the same old practices.

It's simple. The same actions and reactions will only produce variations of the same results and consequences. We call this the "more, better, different" syndrome. "More, better, different" is how we are programmed. It's attractive and has a huge consensus. Who wouldn't want more money, better relationships, and a different job that has no pressure? There's something to be said about "more, better, different," but this quantitative arena is often not the one that affects the quality of your experience. You may in fact find "more, better, different" happening in your life as a result of this process. However, if that is all that happens, you have won the booby prize—it will be an accidental stroke of luck with no solid foundation you can rely on in the future. The purpose of this project is to cause a quantum leap that permanently shifts the quality of your experience of life.

How is this leap different from the "more, better, different" syndrome? "More, better, different" merely entails a change in the contents of your life. The kind of leap we are dedicated to encompasses a shift in the *context* from which you operate—the container in which you hold the specific contents of your life. Not only are you better equipped to change your specific results (to achieve "more, better, different"), but your experience of what can't be changed becomes one of opportunity rather than resignation.

This project clearly aims at more than just getting more of what you now know you want. Beyond improving your current situation, you will develop practices that will dispose you to peak performance permanently and in the face of unforeseen challenges. You will also be contributing to others. Through manifesting your commitment to a quality life, you will contribute to the transformation of the entire planet. You will see how profoundly the world is affected by your presence. It is not necessarily expected, nor desired, for you to change your values. Simply be willing to scrutinize the way your identity has been sculpted through your interpretations and actions, and examine honestly whether that is in line with your vision for your life.

BEING "AT STAKE"

It is one of the facts of life that the most benefits are available through the highest level of participation. "No guts, no glory." Participate every moment as though your life and sanity were at stake. The difference between playing as if your life were at stake, and not playing at that level is well illustrated through this analogy. Bring to mind the last time you were on an airplane. If you had looked around during the emergency procedures instruction, what would you have seen? Most likely, you and your fellow passengers were reading or talking during that part of the flight—in short, you were oblivious to the announcement. Probably you were more concerned with the book you were reading or the person sitting in the next seat than you were about the use of the oxygen mask. Maybe you looked around casually to check where the nearest exit was located, but having flown before, you didn't feel the need to pay much attention to the rest of the information. So far, your flights had all gone smoothly. If something happened, you were certain that you would remember what to do. Now, picture a new scenario. You are in the air. A voice comes over the speaker informing you and your fellow passengers that you have just lost an engine. The flight attendant then begins instructing you according to the same emergency procedures you have heard on countless other flights. How attentive are you this time, and how much more valuable is the experience? The higher the stakes, the more purpose and passion you muster up. That is what I mean when I suggest that you participate as though your life and sanity depend upon it. Not as if you will lose your life or your sanity if you don't participate at this level, but as if what you have to gain by full participation is as precious as life and sanity.

The thought that "One hundred percent is possible one hundred percent of the time" is an empowering source of action. If you live each moment, take each action, speak each word, as though you *could* cause absolutely anything, you will not only feel more alive, but you will be more effective.

URGENCY

If this were the last year of your life, what changes would you be committed to making? With only one year left, what would you want to accomplish in your relationships? Your work life? Your family life?

Your community involvement? The obvious message here is about urgency. There is a saying: Yesterday is a cancelled check; tomorrow a promissory note; the only legal tender is now. Don't wait for something other than your own commitment to put you into action. ("As soon as I get my degree; as soon as I get married; as soon as my kids are grown. . . .") Life for many of us is about getting ready to begin to commence to think about preparing to get started, real soon. Unfortunately, while we are waiting for some person or some event to move us, our own commitment to life remains at least partially dormant. We use similar reasoning retroactively to explain why things haven't turned out the way we wanted them to. ("If only I hadn't gotten married so young; if only I had told the truth sooner; if only my boss had been more understanding. . . .")

Now, these words are not all that new. You may have been asked before about how your life would be different if you had only a short amount of time left. The difference between then and now is that this time you are not requested to simply engage in a reflective process. This time we are talking about committed action and actual results. Part of the process may include some reflection and introspection, but you can count on this process to support and empower you to have your commitments show up in your day-to-day living. Not only will we support you in breaking through to a new level of effective action now, but you will have breakthrough technology available to you forever.

BREAKTHROUGH

Breakthrough is defined as "An act or point of breaking through an obstruction . . . a sudden advance especially in knowledge or technique." In the context of the Basic Training, an obstruction is simply a closure in your life, a possibility that is not available to you now, given how you operate. Einstein's articulation of the theory of relativity was a breakthrough. The facts of the physical universe were no different before Einstein revealed relativity than after. But the possibilities that immediately opened up for humanity were both unprecedented and unpredictable. What had previously been unknown, closed territory for science, was now wide open and available. Similarly, the actual content of your life may not change dramatically in a short period of time (you might have the same job, home, family, body, etc.), but by virtue of the discoveries you make during this process, previously unimaginable advancements will become possible. By breaking through obstructions, we do not mean fixing problems, or uncovering and working on deep-seated psychological blocks. What we do mean is unlocking the gate to higher possibilities than are currently within your reach. Einstein's discovery and thousands of other breakthroughs in music, art, business, the sciences, human relations, and all fields of human endeavor, illustrate that breakthroughs do not only occur in problem areas. You don't have to be doing poorly to get better. Breakthrough is the ticket to excellence at all levels of human progress.

TRANSFORMATION

To *transform* means to change in composition or structure, to change in character or condition, to convert. Thus, a transformation is an act, process, or instance of substantive changing. At the expense of disappointing you, I will tell you that transformation *doesn't* automatically mean changing the content of your life—and, as a by-product of transformation, the content of your life may change. For example, your marriage may improve, you may get that promotion, you may lose weight, you may find yourself attracting more people to you, and so on. But it won't be because you learned "how to" achieve these desired results here. It will be because you experienced transformation— a change of character, condition, composition, or structure.

Certain aspects of human beings can't change—our history, for instance. The extent to which those aspects determine who you are constrains the possibility for change. Therein lies the power of transformation; the possibility of looking at yourself and the world in a new way can liberate you from a fixed, rigid sense of reality—even the aspects of reality that are, in fact, unchangeable.

Another way to say this is that the *context* from which you operate can *always* change even if some of the facts of life cannot. "Context" is the invisible environment, the interrelated conditions, the structure of interpretation in which your life occurs. The context of your life is like water to a fish. The fish doesn't see the water, isn't necessarily aware of the water, doesn't think about the water. And yet, everything in a fish's world is consistent with and generated from the fact that the fish exists in water. Similarly, everything that shows up in your life, every word you speak, and every action you take, is naturally consistent with and indicative of your context.

If you introduce something foreign into an unsupportive context, it will probably not last. For instance, if you plant a fern (content) in the desert (context), it will not live. Likewise, if your general context is joyless, any experiences you have of joy are likely to be rare and temporary. Ferns die in the desert, and joy can't thrive in a joyless context. People who function from a context of scarcity typically do not have enough money, time, friends, confidence, education, and so on, to accomplish their dreams. Conversely, those who operate from a context of abundance typically generate the resources to manifest their commitments. Why? It can't always be explained by analyzing the circumstances. Often, those who have the least conducive circumstances end up unpredictably successful, and those with all the resources to begin with don't make it. That indicates that there is something beyond or underneath the content—circumstances—that, to a great degree, determines what is possible for someone. It isn't pure luck or talent that permits some people to succeed consistently regardless of the circumstances, while others fail. The good news is that you can shift your context, thereby reshaping your possibilities. That is what we call transformation.

The content of your life gives you valuable information about the context from which you live. However, the most effective way to generate change is by transformation—a conversion of the *context* that dictates your actions.

Transformation does not imply a need to change your fundamental principles. If you are not clear about your principles, you have the opportunity here to get clear, to declare, what you stand for as a human being. Then, you can explore whether or not you have a context established that generates actions that support your stand.

YOUR PURPOSE

This process is about everything crucial to adult life that you weren't taught in school. What are your goals from this opportunity? In what areas of your life are you looking for new possibilities, new accomplishments? Maybe you intend to give new meaning to your relationships (marriage, family, social, business, community, with yourself); maybe you want to advance your communication skills, your business performance; maybe you want to get clear about your goals, address a management problem, or complete a specific project you've been grappling with. Take time to reflect on your vision of the value you could generate through this vehicle.

If you look at life from a black-or-white perspective, you'll see that you either have the results you say you want, or all the reasons why not. It's binary and it's deceptively simple. Reasons or results. All of us have mastered rationalization and justification because of our need to be right, our need to cover up the consequences of our actions. It is automatic for us to give reasons and explanations in all situations. Reasons, in a sense, have us.

Human beings are particularly resourceful and tenacious about finding reasons to explain why we don't do what we say we are going to do. The good news about reasons is that they make you feel good, or let you be right, at least in the short run. Reasons, rationalizations, and justifications disguise the simple fact that you didn't do what you said you would or wanted to do. You or someone else is still left dealing with the facts, regardless of how adept you are at justifying and deflecting your accountability.

Here are some questions and suggestions to assist you in beginning to explore this in your own life. Write your responses down in your journal.

- When you break your word and don't do something you said you would do, what excuses do you most frequently give? Where or on whom do you place the blame—yourself; your boss; the economy; your parents; your children; sudden, unexpected circumstances; not having the time; other?
- Consider that you only use those reasons to cover up something. What might it be?
- What would it take from you, and what would you gain, from being able to say simply 'I'm sorry. I didn't get it done'? This week, try to dispense with your reasons.
- What would it take from you, and what would you gain from being able to decline the unwanted requests of others without explaining your refusal? Try it this week.
- What reasons are you likely to come up with if you don't accomplish what you say you want out of reading this book?

Let's address your specific concerns. What is going on in your life right now? What is next for you? Why are you reading this book? Write your thoughts in your journal.

The Constitution of the United States, which was written out of respect for the dignity of the individual and our system, is structured to protect and ensure individual liberty. However, there is no guarantee that you will have the courage to exercise your liberties in ways consonant with your highest aspirations and in accordance with the maximum benefit to society. Lifespring is dedicated to opening these possibilities to you, to turning abstract political rights into genuine personal accomplishments. Engaging in this inquiry can't guarantee that you will succeed, in an objective sense, in everything you do, but our work together can empower you to take the necessary risks and to participate with all you've got—to take full advantage of your freedom. There are very few events that can intervene in your life the way the kind of commitment we are discussing in these pages can—to enable you to act on the aspirations expressed in our Constitution.

You have the opportunity to see where you are, where you want to be headed, and where you are going to end up given the direction you are heading now. Participating one hundred percent in this exercise involves risk. Exploring the topics raised here provides a kind of laboratory where you can play out your risk taking. These aren't undo risks—they don't threaten your physical or psychological well-being. You risk identifying the inauthentic self-image you project to others. You risk having to take a real stand—a stand demonstrated in your actions—either for or against the ideals that you claim to endorse.

Your investment of time, energy, and money will only generate progress for you if you are motivated by a commitment to truly get something done in your life. This book can be a vehicle for your accomplishment. But it cannot cause anything in your life. Only you cause action in your life. This inquiry is an opportunity for you to clarify your principles, priorities, and goals, and to break through in your ability to express yourself authentically, powerfully, and effectively.

This book is about your life. It is not full of answers, contains no easy steps to happiness, and will not instruct you in a technique for "how to" improve yourself. The possibilities this book opens up for you will come out of your own commitment to changing your practices. The promises I make to you are that our interaction will further the commitment you have to your life, will transform your sense of peace and well-being, and that through your participation you will significantly increase your ability to act effectively and produce the results you say you want.

A word that has been played down so far is "fulfillment." What good would self-examination be if it didn't result in fulfillment? Fulfillment is a matter of interpretation, a personal issue. For my money, fulfillment is born out of passion, commitment, and effective action. I assert that if you are committed to living as though your life actually depends on it, you will be fulfilled.

Let's look at the reasons you decided to give this book a chance. Maybe you are a graduate of the Lifespring courses. Maybe a friend has been trying to get you to take a Lifespring course and this is your compromise. Maybe you devour "self-help" books. Maybe you want to prove to yourself once and for all that Lifespring is a fraud. Maybe you are just curious.

There is nothing wrong with those reasons, but a commitment to curiosity, or to obtaining information, or to satisfying a friend, or to being right, will not get anything accomplished in your life. From this point on, I request that you read as though something in your life were really at stake. Naturally, you are free to decline my request—but what if something here could actually enhance your life? Who would be losing? Allow for the possibility that this experience *may* be a catalyst for making an extraordinary difference in your own life.

Consider the questions posed below, and, out of your commitment to accomplishment, take action. I recommend, once again, recording your thoughts in your journal.

- What is your purpose in reading this book?
- What is *really* your purpose in reading this book?
- If you accomplished the breakthroughs you are aiming for, specifically how would they affect your life?
- What is the effective action you need to take to accomplish what you say you want?
- What is your vision for your future?
- What is missing or what is needed to accomplish that vision?

GRADUATE PROFILE

Helen Shreves is an attorney, wife, and mother of two, living in Denver, Colorado. She first did the Basic Training in 1984. In looking back at her training experience, Helen recounts that "prior to the trainings, one of the things I would do in my life to not be intimate with people is that I would be very judgmental. At the time I took the training I was feeling very critical of people. I would judge anyone I met consciously or subconsciously. I'd register if they had been to college, if they were bright, what kind of clothes they wore—were the fabrics expensive, were they successful, were they unemployed? I could categorize people very rapidly. I like you.

I don't like you. My posture going into the Basic Training was sort of sitting back, with my arms crossed, looking at people thinking, 'Jesus, get your act together!'

"If you asked anyone who knew me before the training, they would say that I was a happy person. I've always been a happy person, a good mood–type person. But, I was not being vulnerable. I was trying to be superwoman—a wonderful mother, a trial lawyer, president of the Colorado Women's Bar Association. I didn't need anybody. The result was this feeling of separateness. I felt separateness from the people in my family, my colleagues, any group I was part of.

"I'm not a shy person, so it's not a matter of not being shy. I have no problems with talking in front of a group, or anything like that. My breakthrough was more about not criticizing and judging others. By jumping into the training, participating with those people in the group, I was saying that I was a part of them. I was not different, or better, or smarter, or comparing myself to them in any way. I was just part of a group, one of the gang. I let myself be part of a group. I was not analyzing, being critical or judging so much. People in my small group and others who knew me noticed it. And outside the training, I stopped being critical of my husband; I am accepting him as a worthy person.

"One of the major distinctions that came out of the training was seeing that being warm, loving, and vulnerable is powerful. My power doesn't lie in pushiness or hardness. You see, in the legal world, it's accepted for a woman to be a 'tough broad.' That's who they want to hire. In that field, I could act it out like you can't believe. The problem was that I confused being a tough lawyer with being a powerful woman. I discovered that what lets people in and brings them close to me is being warm and loving with them. Being that way is powerful and strong.

I am naturally a very energetic and outward-focused person. When I left the training, I was very centered. Very focused. Very soft, I guess you could say. It was really a good balance. It has been an incredibly valuable process of accepting and integrating different kinds of power and strength, of not worrying if this person thinks I'm a bitch, and that person thinks I am weak.

"An example of that from a training was an exercise in which the group was presented with a problem to solve. I immediately stood up and said that we should decide the issue with a vote. Well, some men in the group were extremely put off by me. They told me to sit down and shut up. Finally, nothing having been accomplished, the trainer came over and pointed out that I had suggested the correct method in the first place. She pointed out how the men had reacted to me like I was being a righteous bitch. So, we all learned. It really made a difference for a couple of the men who learned something about how they interacted with women. And I saw what I evoke in men when I behave in certain ways. I think I was intimidating.

"The training was about taking both sides of me and putting them together—like a dual thing of letting my strength blossom, and yet learning how to do it in a way that brings warmth and vulnerability to it. After the trainings, I really felt a flowering of myself in many areas. I came out of the training balanced and softened, and also having released a lot of energy.

"A great deal of creativity started as soon as I completed the training. For example, I painted some canvases that still hang here in my home. I was not an artist and had not painted before. The only way I could have painted those was because I was different; I had gotten in touch with a different part of myself that had never been touched before. My creativity also exploded in my professional life. I put together a videotape on how to do your own noncontested divorce which is now in the Denver Public Library, and is watched all the time. I developed a restraining order packet with another woman lawyer—thousands of them have been sold. I put information together for the family law section of the library including a resource directory of experts to use in doing a divorce case. Law isn't the most creative field, and many lawyers never even think about doing anything like those projects. I think I have been about as creative as anyone can be.

"The first few days of the training, I just sat back watching it, analyzing it. I eventually shared in front of the group on Saturday morning, after which time I participated a lot. A big process for me was when I looked at commitments, specifically breaking commitments. At that time, I would break a lot of commitments to my daughter, who was then twelve. I would say that I would be home at a certain time, and then I'd always take one more call, making myself late. I think I have always been good with little children. But when my daughter started getting older, I pulled back a little bit. I put distance between us and was judging whether I thought she was doing things right or not. That was very painful for me to look at, but taking that kind of honest look has improved our relationship significantly. I have made time with her, kept my promises to her, talked with her, been physically warm with her. She has really felt big changes in me.

"Another thing that was very big for me was looking at accountability and not blaming or trying to change others. I think about that a lot in my own life because, being a lawyer, I'm in a man's world. I had problems with men, as I have mentioned, because I was showing up like the kind of woman men experience as a righteous bitch. Before the training, I tended to blame the difficulties on the men, or on the social structure. After the training, I experienced a tremendous decrease in my level of anger toward others. I am much more honest with people in my life and it's had tremendous benefits. I have stopped manipulating people to get what I want. I had been trying to change them, but now I'm just straightforward with them.

"My performance at work was noticeably enhanced after the Basic Training. For example, just before taking the Basic Training I had started a custody trial. I did two days of hearings the week before the Basic started and then the case was put off until a few months later. We ended up having the last two days of hearings a couple of months after I did the training. At the end of the first day of the second session of hearings my client stopped me and said 'Jesus, what happened to you? You were so fabulous in there!' I realized that I had this ability to organize better, focus better, and had all this renewed energy. I've always been a good lawyer, but I remember during those hearings just sitting back and looking at it differently, having a bigger picture of what I wanted to get accomplished, and being more effective at getting that done.

"Another example is that I have always been such an action person, I've always hated to sit down and write. A couple of months ago I agreed to speak at a seminar. I sat down one day, thought about it, and wrote out a really good outline. I was focused, I was organized, I didn't procrastinate, and I completed a good work product substantially before it was due. I can honestly say that I generally wouldn't have been able to organize my time and thinking as effectively before the trainings.

"My increased ability to concentrate has been apparent in many different circumstances; at social events, business functions, seminars. I'm still very energetic, but I am able to sit down, focus, and keep my concentration steady for long periods of time, which before would have been out of the question."

Helen's relationship with her husband has been affected by their participation in the training. "My relationship with my husband has changed and I would never go back to the relationship we had before. We are spending more time talking, and I am risking and saying things I wouldn't have said before for fear he would disapprove. I have always worried about disapproval from men. Not worrying so much about disapproval has affected all of my interactions with both men and women. They are more honest, more gratifying.

"One unexpected thing that I saw in the training was how I had suppressed my sensuality. I was holding back, not giving it much energy. I had started to feel dowdy. I realized, after the training, that I can be feminine, wear feminine clothes, *and* be very powerful and businesslike. I have started to act more feminine and soft and I feel wonderful about my femininity and sensuality.

"The training was a life-changing process. There is no doubt about that. And I can never go back. The same things happen in life, but I don't react the same way I used to. I am so empowered, effective and fulfilled."

Ways We Create Value / Ways We Avoid

4

WAYS WE CREATE VALUE

You can increase your ability to learn from life by participating proactively. By doing certain things, you can turn life into an ever-expanding, adventurous, active learning experience. This section puts forth recommendations regarding how you can maximize your ability to learn both from the experience of reading this book, and from your most valuable teachers: your own life and the people in your life.

Full participation is the first key to creating value. The value for you in reading this book will come from applying what you read to your participation in life. Ironically, the most valuable part of this process will not happen while you are reading. You will gain substantive value only when you apply your discoveries and insights to your daily practices. The formula is simple—the more you get involved in this project, the more you will profit. Participation, not for the sake of participation, but in order to have something extraordinary happen in your life, is a key ingredient in the effectiveness of this (or any) process.

Does this mean that you should agree with everything written here? Not necessarily. It really doesn't matter if you believe or agree with any of this because the goal is not to replace your belief system with another one. The aim instead is to have you experience some powerful possibilities that exist *outside* of your belief system, possibilities that are closed to you unless you embrace the opportunity to live outside of the comfort and security of your beliefs. You may challenge some of your beliefs and the assumptions you have about yourself, the world, and other people. Again, the purpose is not to convince you that your beliefs are wrong, but to reveal your current structure of interpretation, thus providing an opening for breakthrough.

It is human to be skeptical, but if you are determined to hang on fixedly to your current ways of being, then you cannot create anything new. For many of us our stubbornness is a source of pride, strength, uniqueness. However, an unwillingness to consider the possibility that there may be different, more productive, and fulfilling ways to be, will obstruct your attempts to attain greater results both in this project and in life in general. Of course we all like to be right, but investment in being right is a dead end. Only open-mindedness will support you in achieving extraordinary results.

Risking, moving out of the security of your "comfort zone," is another way to create value. Your comfort zone is the level of participation in life that is comfortable for you. It encompasses those ways of being that are habitual and do not involve personal risk or challenge. Your comfort zone is where you operate the majority of the time. You probably look pretty good and feel pretty happy when you are operating at about 40 to 60 percent of your maximum commitment and effectiveness. That is your comfort zone. It both describes your standard operating procedures and defines the boundaries that you are not likely to risk traversing.

Risk, the possibility of loss or injury, is something that human beings expend a lot of energy, and suppress a lot of creativity, to avoid. Whether it be physical, financial, or interpersonal risk, we are, for the most part, strongly inclined to eliminate the chance of suffering any loss or injury, even at the reciprocal cost of narrowing our possibilities for being. Without willingness to risk, there is no possibility. We as Americans have a concept of possibility, but we can't experience it unless we learn to take the appropriate risks.

Since the training is designed specifically as a supportive environment for appropriate risk taking, most participants venture to levels of honesty, openness, commitment, spontaneity and self-expression beyond anything they had formerly experienced. For you, alone with this book, it will take more personal commitment and courage to create the same value. Why? Simply because you do not now have the advantage of beginning in the supportive environment of the training room with others who are committed to your commitment. When the training is over and it is time to return back to everyday life, graduates face a moment to moment choice whether they will step outside their comfort zones and create the same degree of value where it really counts—with their families, careers, marriages, communities, and so on. You, however, must confront that choice on your own from the start.

The essence of our work is to allow you to step out a bit on the edge, the edge of what you know and are comfortable with, the edge of certainty. Permit yourself to—I won't say "enjoy"—risk, but to make risk permissible, to have risk become an "of course" in your life rather than something you spend all your energy trying to avoid.

Why risk if you are truly comfortable and your life is working just as it is? What exactly is the appeal and value of risking and moving outside your comfort zone? Will you have a more meaningful experience of life if you strive to be *un*comfortable? You probably wouldn't be reading this book in the first place if you didn't have at least an inkling regarding the answers to these questions. When it comes right down to it, only you can answer them for yourself. There is no objective reason for risking out of your comfort zone. In fact, for every argument for the power of risking and extending yourself beyond the limitations of your comfort zone, there is a counterargument in favor of staying within the boundaries of comfort. For instance, there are enlivening advantages in operating on the edge of personal risk. You accomplish more than you ever imagined possible; you continually become more effective; you attract people who are alive and purposeful; you have a sense of making a real difference to people. But the reality is that in addition to the personal rewards you gain by traveling outside your comfort zone, you may pay prices: You may, at times, look foolish or encounter criticism; you may experience hurt or loss; your expectations of yourself may increase; others may increase their expectations of you; you may have to learn to deal with greater degrees of success and failure; and so on. Think about your own life. Only you know what specific rewards lie outside your comfort zone and what prices you will have to pay to attain those rewards.

Take a moment to again question your motives for reading this book. Clarity of purpose is a critical element of a coherent, directed inquiry. Write your thoughts in your journal.

- Are you really ready and willing to explore what is available to you outside of your comfort zone?
- What do you want to accomplish by embarking on this adventure?
- Are you prepared to pay the prices that may be part of that journey?
- Do you have a sense of how your personal transformation fits into your larger vision for your future?

Honesty will support you in accomplishing your goals with integrity. Be direct and tell the truth to yourself and others. We all know that "honesty is the best policy," but often we are less than truthful, either by omission or by commission. Not that you should bare your soul to the dry cleaner or the grocery checker just because they say "Hi, how are you?," but stop and look before you throw out the usual "Fine, thanks, how are you?" If you're fabulous or awful instead of fine, it will serve you to be in recognition of the truth. Your automatic conversations often cover up important information. You are at least one step removed from taking effective action if you aren't communicating authentically. Practice this yourself. In the next couple of days, when someone asks you how you are doing, tell them how you are *really* doing, using adjectives that are outside of your usual repertoire. See what happens for you.

Your principles and commitments will guide you in your honesty. Sometimes being honest just for the sake of being honest just doesn't serve. For instance, "Grandma, you look ugly today" doesn't work. There are times, however, when you withhold, censor, or temper your communications to the detriment of the work at hand. Merely because honesty is uncomfortable for you is not a reason to be dishonest if speaking the truth will benefit those involved in the long run.

Consider that even when you don't come out and tell the truth about something, others "get it" anyway. Use any relationship as an example. If you are angry at someone, but don't confront them, doesn't your anger get expressed in less direct ways? If you are sorry about something, but don't apologize, doesn't your guilt show up anyway? If you are attracted to someone, but don't muster up the courage to do anything about it, don't you think your attraction is obvious in subtle ways? We have a million ways of getting our message across if it is important to us to be heard. One way or the other, the truth will be known. There are several problems with being indirect, or covert, about communicating the truth. First, it is disrespectful. It is like telling someone he or she isn't worth the risk of being honest. Second, it thwarts opportunities for dealing directly with the issue at hand in the first place. You are merely getting revenge, or getting attention, without giving the other person a chance to address the issue directly. Third, you are closing down possibilities available for you with that person. Until you complete unfinished business, that incompletion will hinder your freedom to interact with that person. Fourth, you are not expressing yourself in a way that has you be known. It is as simple as telling the truth, yet almost nothing in life takes as much courage.

So far we have identified: *full participation, an open mind, risking, clarity of purpose,* and *honesty*. The list could go on to include trust, spontaneity, acceptance, and others. What it takes, at the root level, for you to accomplish extraordinary things is a *commitment* to your own transformation.

The only way to play at life that will ensure maximum results is to participate as though you were the quarterback and your job is on the line with every play. Expand the stakes to include your family, your health, your marriage, your wealth, your spiritual development; everything is on the line and depends on your participation. A player on the field knows that he has to give it his all because he will personally take the consequences no matter what happens. A committed player plays one hundred percent. A second-string player is still on the team and is intent on winning the game, but his personal stake isn't as high, and his participation does not require or demonstrate as high a gradient of commitment as the player on the field. The fans are also participating as enthusiasts and supporters, but no matter how faithful they are, they know that they will be going home at the end of the game, their lives basically unaffected by the outcome of the game. The consequences they will pay if their team loses are substantially different than the players' consequences. In the press box, reporters play observers, critics, narrators. Other than their personal loyalties, the reporters have no investment in which team wins or in which players score touchdowns. The absurd and ironic truth is that we *often* don't participate in our lives with as much commitment as players on the field in a game of football. Notice how often you play second-string, or fan, or reporter in your own life.

Answer the following questions about your participation. Use your journal.

- How have you participated in this inquiry so far? Have you been a committed player, an observer, a critic, a dreamer . . . ?
- How will you know if you are participating with a commitment to getting something done in your life? What is the specific, measurable evidence you can look for?
- What is it that you want to accomplish and how have you approached that intention so far?
- What are the risks for you in being honest and direct with yourself and others, and what are the benefits?

WAYS WE AVOID

Each of us has a whole catalog of clever methods for concealing that we are not participating fully in our lives. These methods are the ways we avoid. We have been well-conditioned throughout our lives to avoid one hundred percent participation in many areas of our lives, and equally encouraged to perpetuate the illusion that we are participating fully. We have learned not to expose ourselves while appearing to be open. At a very meaningful level these mechanisms evoke dissatisfaction and unfulfillment, and are obstacles to creating value.

The many dangers of avoidance boil down to sabotage—avoidance is self-sabotage. Avoidance leaves incompletions which, in turn, hinder further action. You are not really "present" as energy is diverted from fulfilling your commitments to serving the cause of avoidance. You become an obstacle to your own progress rather than a contributor. Your behavior is part of the problem rather than part of the solution. Whether you are avoiding little details or major projects, by avoiding, you sabotage the very areas of concern in which you are committed to success.

How often do you hear people tell their kids: "If you don't have anything nice to say, don't say anything at all," "Don't get so excited," "If you are going to cry, go to your room," "Don't talk about that in front of other people," etc., etc., etc.? It's a safe bet that you were given an array of such advice. Typically, kids are rewarded for behavior that suits their parents' perception of what is right, even though it seems to be inauthentic for the child. Of course, being a parent is a complex responsibility, part of which involves teaching our children values and coaching them about what works and what doesn't. Parents are not at fault, they are simply perpetuating the culture's shared understanding of how people are. Unfortunately, some elements of the cultural framework limit you by accepting, and even encouraging, you to be incomplete and to avoid responsibility.

Your cultural background and mores are inescapable and it is impossible to nullify their influence on you. What you can do is begin to recognize how your particular culture—race, religion, ethnic origin, language, traditions, social and economic factors—dictates your actions, and develop practices within that context which allow you to be effective. Recognizing how you avoid and learning how to interrupt your automatic behavior patterns gives you freedom where you might otherwise be unconsciously restricted.

Why do we avoid? We are trained from an early age not to let ourselves be vulnerable, to insulate ourselves from personal threat. We keep ourselves from becoming involved in situations which may threaten us or leave us vulnerable.

How do we manifest this in our behavior? Some of our favorite avoidances include ignoring what is going on, spacing out, reading, taking drugs, getting angry, watching TV, being a workaholic, drinking alcohol, eating, getting sick, laughing, delegating, being confused, lying, over-analyzing, rationalizing, doing busy work, running away, going to the bathroom, denying reality, hesitating, sleeping, talking, fantasizing, making lists, smoking cigarettes, or otherwise procrastinating. Some of these avoidance behaviors are airtight defenses. Who would dare blame you for working so hard? It's the American way! Who would complain that your hysterical sense of humor is distracting? A great sense of humor is always at the top of the list of qualities we like in people. Or who would think that you are avoiding an issue, given how much time and energy you spend analyzing and figuring it out?

Does this mean that every time you watch TV, go to the bathroom, or get sick you are avoiding something? Not necessarily. But the bad news is that our avoidances are so ingrained in our behavior that we are often not aware of when we are avoiding and when we are simply watching TV.

Consider the following questions to assist you in clarifying your avoidance patterns.

- What situations are stressful for you?
- What behaviors do you commonly exhibit in those situations?
- How do you alleviate your discomfort or make yourself invulnerable to further discomfort?
- What are your most common avoidance mechanisms?
- What are you avoiding? What is the worst thing you can imagine happening if you were to face the situations head on?

Why not avoid? It seems expedient to eliminate the discomfort of facing up to unpleasantness. For one thing, you lose much of the texture of your life by staying safe, not going out on a limb for anything, making sure that you always look good; the range of experiences open to you is limited. Avoidance blurs the distinct significance of different things, events, and people. Life becomes a bland concoction of safe activities and relationships, none much more meaningful than any other. Do you ever notice that when you say something really matters to you and throw yourself into it, you experience a high level of aliveness and passion? Whereas, when you say that something matters to you but don't really put yourself at stake, you lack passion, regardless of whether you succeed or not.

Avoidance affects our relationships deeply by detaching us from others. As we go through life covering up the fact that we are in avoidance, we gesture at getting involved with people and projects while skillfully keeping ourselves safe and, therefore, fundamentally uninvolved. When you are not authentically involved in your projects and interactions, you are not fully available to others either to communicate your concerns to them or to let their concerns touch you. The moving experience of partnership, of making a difference with another human being, is blocked as your focus is on yourself alone.

You've begun to look at your avoidance mechanisms and why you avoid. Now move to the next step and use your journal to explore how avoidance affects your life:

- What prices do you pay in your relationships because of your particular avoidance pattern?

- Remember some specific instances in which you recently avoided something. What motivated your avoidance? What are some of the opportunities you missed by doing that? What are other consequences of your avoidance?

Are you having a hard time seeing how you avoid: identifying your "favorite" avoidance behaviors; remembering times when you were avoiding? If yes, consider the possibility that you are avoiding telling yourself the truth. No matter how passionate and involved you are in your life, you are human. And human beings avoid. It's up to you. To create forward movement, you must tell yourself the truth and then dig deeper to find what's next for you.

Bill Garrett

5

GRADUATE PROFILE

Bill Garrett is an emergency physician in Denver, Colorado. "Now I deal with patients as people whereas before I dealt with people as patients. It is very easy for people who are attracted to medicine, who are very scientific and analytical in their orientation—like myself—to fall into a trap, a mechanism of living and dealing with patients that is very structured. The medical literature decries the doctors who refer to their patients as 'The broken ankle,' 'The headache,' 'Room 12,' or whatever. But, before the Basic Training that was very real for me. People were patients, diseases. In the Basic Training I began to realize that I wasn't dealing with disease, I was dealing with people who are diseased. I began to identify ways in which physicians could be healers in a different sense than simply giving medication, making diagnoses, prescribing therapies. There is more to healing than making people symptom free.

"Now, I look at my patients as *people*. I approach them from a more holistic perspective. It's important to me how their home life is, how their social life is, whether they smoke or don't smoke, whether they use drugs or alcohol excessively. I deal with them accountably about all of that. Are they aware of what they are doing, of the impact their actions have on them, that they are the ones choosing those things? I introduce the concepts of choice, of accountability. It's a challenge for me not to be judgmental about it and to communicate in a way that they don't feel like I am judging them, but to make the point that there is a possibility that their symptoms may be a reflection of something else going on in their lives. Many people haven't considered that they may have something to do with being ill, and conversely, with being well.

"When I did the Basic in 1984, I went in there very judgmental—assessing and intellectualizing everything. I can remember sitting near the back of the room saying to myself, 'I know what's going on here.' I sat back there analyzing and figuring out the first couple of days. Then, people's sharing started having an impact on me. I found myself crying or laughing, very attuned to what was going on with each person sharing. When I finished the training I felt like a weight had been lifted off my shoulders. My judgments of people just faded. During one exercise on Saturday, when I just looked into one person's eyes after another's, I had the experience of compassion, of feeling from their perspective more than my own. And I noticed that things like clothing, hair, and appearance just did not matter. A lot of my judgments had been based on physical or material considerations before then. On that day, those priorities were simply eliminated.

"I would say that, professionally, the most significant impact the trainings have had is in my listening to my patients. Before Lifespring, my approach was power oriented. It was: address the patient, establish that I'm the doctor and they're the patient as quickly as I can, assess their symptoms and physical findings so that I can make a diagnosis, make the diagnosis, and then plug that into some formula that says how to treat that condition. I was very successful at treating diseases, but not as competent at relating to the patients as human beings. Since the trainings, I listen to my patients and I use a lot more intuition in dealing with people.

"An example is one of my patients—a woman about twenty-two years old. She was visiting her mother from out of state. She came into the emergency department complaining of abdominal pain. She was lying there on the stretcher writhing in pain and vomiting. I went over and introduced myself and tried to calm her. We ran all of the appropriate tests for that kind of problem. The results were all normal. I sat down with her and said, 'Well, I have all the tests back and they're all normal. That doesn't mean that there's nothing wrong with you, but I don't know what's wrong with you. Do you have any idea?' She broke into tears. She just sobbed. Now, back before the trainings I probably would have said, 'Now, come on, try to control yourself. Let's figure out what's going on here.' But instead, I just let her cry and I think I even held her hand. I asked her, 'What do you think is going on?' It turned out that she had come to visit her mother because her husband had been beating her. She was thinking of leaving her husband. Her mother was very critical of her, basically taking the husband's side. While we were talking about it, her pain went away, right there in the emergency department. She recognized that her abdominal pain was a reaction to much more significant things in her life than a health problem. Well, before the afternoon was out, her mother and her husband and she and I sat down and talked. We addressed this problem of physical and emotional abuse and discussed how they were really not loving each other and caring for each other. Before the trainings I probably would have paid more attention to the test results than to her as a person.

"Then there was another woman, a little bit older, who came in absolutely insistent that there was something wrong with her. I examined her and, again, everything was normal. I did many more tests than I would normally do in the emergency department—I think because I was really listening to her. I just knew that she was telling the truth, or I assumed it and operated from that perspective. Although there was no evidence from the examination and the tests, in listening to her I was convinced that something was going on. I didn't know what it was and that didn't matter. Before the training I might have just told her that we couldn't find any problem, dismissed her, and told her to go home and come back if it didn't go away. This time, though, I discussed it with her private physcian, and he agreed to put her into the hospital and do more investigation. About six days later she came down to the emergency room dressed in a hospital gown. She walked up, gave me a big hug, and thanked me for believing in her and listening to her. A day or so after she had entered the hospital, they had found a tumor in her pelvis. She had been to surgery a couple of days later to remove the tumor. They caught it before it had spread to any other organs or glands, and early enough that she would be cured. That case shows the difference made by listening to people, by taking into consideration that they do have the capacity to know their level of health at any given time. That has had a dramatic impact on my relationship with my patients.

"Another way that there is a difference in my practice is in dealing with death. I deal with a lot of death in the emergency room. Very frequently it's unexpected death. I work in a community that is relatively young—25 percent of our patient population is less than fourteen years of age. We consequently see a lot of sudden infant death syndrome. Some time after I did the training, a seven-month-old child was brought in dead. The parents were understandably distraught. My way of dealing with this in the past was to build barriers and to shield myself, protect myself and my emotions, and not to share those with anybody. Death was simply a fact of life—it was part of my job to deal with it. I developed my own mechanisms for dealing with it mentally at home. That resulted in a lack of sensitivity, a short temperedness, and so on. But, when this child came in I actually went to the mother and put my arm around her. I cried with her. I dealt with the real emotional, human part of medicine. The mother was comfortable enough in that situation to actually put her arm around me and to cry on my shoulder. That never would have happened before. I would have been so rigid and cold and unemotional that there wouldn't have been space for that to happen. It was very significant to me to have this mother be willing to share her grief and to feel comfortable sharing my own empathy.

"In addition to working with patients, I work with a lot of physicians. I am medical director for the emergency department of this hospital with seven physicians working as a team. I'm also the regional medical director for a large emergency medicine company based in Florida, with hospitals in Chicago, Toledo, St. Louis, and here in Denver. Also, I'm the medical director for Adolph Coors Company. There are over twenty physicians that I am directly responsible for at different hospitals. I credit the Basic Training with a change in my management style. Prior to the training my management style was highly structured and rule-oriented. At this point, I am open to possibilities rather than being positioned on my opinion about how it has to be. Creativity and expression of feelings are important to me now. I allow the doctors more of an opportunity to participate in my meetings, rather than just focusing on what *I* want to get done. That has resulted in the doctors calling me more often to talk and explore possibilities. Before I was very rarely called on by them.

"Also, I have been more effective in dealing with stress and in helping other doctors deal with stress. The opportunity for stress is certainly present in medicine. Before I would cover up my stress, but usually it would still bubble inside me and just show up some other way. Now, I take an action-oriented approach to stress. I recognize it, and do something about its cause. I have been able to help other doctors deal with their stress. In working with other doctors, again, I think it's a matter of listening. I listen to these doctors as human beings; they feel safe being with me, and can really be open and honest, thereby identifying the source of their stress and possible solutions.

"The trainings had an impact across the board: in my practice, my marriage, and my family. I had always told myself that I didn't want to have kids. I had a great rationalization about how they were too distracting from the other commitments in my life, and just not worth the effort. During a revealing exercise during the training, I realized that I was using those stories as excuses not to have children because I was afraid to be a father. There was really something there that I had been covering up and pretending was something else. We now have a nineteen-month-old daughter.

"My wife and I did the Lifespring trainings together. That was a real challenge, but it was a way that we could demonstrate our commitment to honest communication and to sharing. I deal with conflict in our relationship differently now. At one point in time, conflict was the worst thing in the world. I avoided it at all costs. When I was in conflict with someone, something was terribly wrong. Now it's an opportunity for looking, for exploring. Conflict doesn't carry with it all of the negativity, guilt, and anger it used to. In fact, I actually get almost excited about it now that I have the ability to refocus whatever we're in conflict about and put it into a constructive perspective. At one time it was a matter of avoiding or preventing conflict. Now it's a matter of looking at conflict as an opportunity to take some action, to create something different. I would say that through the courses I got to understand for myself what marriage is—and perhaps what marriage is not.

"There have also been very dramatic changes in my relationships with my sister and brother. To put it succinctly, I feel like I have a real brother for the first time in my life. Until we both did the trainings—he finally did them a couple of years after I did—you could describe our relationship as 'sibling rivalry.' Right after I did the training, I told him 'You've got to do this training. I just want you to do this training.' Well, thanks to my approaching him that way, he had great resolve *never* to do this training. My sister did the training without much resistance. By now, most of the family has done it. Last Christmas, both of them came out with their entire families. We spent the holidays acknowledging what we were thankful for in our lives, and acknowledging each other. There isn't a chance that we would have done anything like that before. My brother and I used to talk on the phone maybe twice a year. And those conversations were very formal and mechanical. The degree of love and caring that we have demonstrated since the trainings is miraculous.

"Relationships was a huge part of the training for me—relationships with my wife, family, patients, and colleagues. I saw how I would manipulate relationships. I realized that power—being powerful—doesn't necessarily mean being in control. Someone doesn't have to be in control for there to be an effective relationship. In my relationships with my patients, my wife, my little girl, my parents and the rest of my family, there has been a significant shift in my concept of power. There simply *is* power in relationship, it isn't power *over* anything. There is power in the people. If there is winning, it is in expressing power not in *having* power. That has transformed my relationships and my life.

Can People Really Transform?

6

How many classes have you taken, or books have you read for the purpose of getting better at something? How much time, energy, and money have you invested in improving certain specific skills or qualities (i.e., time management courses, assertiveness trainings, skiing lessons, management technique seminars, weight control, piano or ballet lessons, financial planning lectures)? What long-term results came out of those courses or books? What did your investment actually yield? Are you consistently applying what you learned in your daily practices?

The point in asking these questions is not to debunk these kinds of learning. There is definitely a place in our lives for skill-specific, informational, or technical education. In fact, one of the most critical steps to becoming an expert at almost anything, whether it be skiing or management, is to be coached in the specific skills and attitudes of mastery in that particular field. Then, you must surrender or put aside what you think you already know and be open to this coaching. Being coached means subordinating yourself to the experts such that they are able to intervene in, correct, and help you refine your practices so that you become more effective. By "subordinating yourself" I mean submitting to the guidance of another, following their instructions even if you don't understand the reason or if they seem illogical to you—barring anything illegal or immoral. Look at all the programs you have taken with the intention of becoming better at something. Did those courses fulfill their promise? Did the effect last? Predictably, you probably did not integrate the new information into your practice in a way that made a lasting difference.

In Lifespring courses improved effectiveness is not the direct purpose but a by-product of a broader transformation in your personal commitment to having your life and the world work. Actual results and measurable progress in specific projects are important. In fact, the very reason Lifespring is so successful is that graduates do experience significant, tangible improvement in specific areas of their lives—and their return on investment increases over time. Transformational training has the added benefit of potentially affecting *all* areas of your life; the practices of breakthrough are not limited to one specific skill or ability.

THE FIXED SELF

Perhaps you're thinking: "Of course, who wouldn't want transformation and breakthrough? But come on, people are who they are. Some things just don't change. How can you suggest that people can fundamentally 'transform' even if they wanted to?" If so, your skepticism illuminates an historical philosophical dilemma. Is there something fixed, concrete, and unchangeable about human beings, or is it actually possible for individuals to make essential shifts in their way of being?

Logically, transformation is only possible if you have an understanding of human beings that is consistent with transformation. The understanding that prevails in our society today is the view that self is basically "fixed"; that our identities are comprised of static qualities and characteristics over which we have little control, but that play a leading role in how our lives turn out. We act like we were just born shy, outgoing, interesting, boring, whimsical, serious, ambitious, lazy, committed, flaky; that's the way we are and the way we will always be. That understanding does not leave much of an opening for the possibility of transformation. Those characterizations can be road-blocks to breakthrough in that they preclude any possibilities that are not consonant with them. While degrees of improvement are certainly possible, at the bottom of this view is a mood of resignation to the inevitable which undermines any hope of unpredictable breakthrough.

What basis is there for the claim that such characteristics are, in fact, fixed? When a surgeon opens up a patient for an operation, does he or she find shyness or laziness or funniness inside the patient's body? Of course not. Those characterizations are 100 percent interpretation. We can usually point to evidence that will support our character-izations of ourselves and others. However, none of that evidence can objectively stand on its own as proof of a fixed self; all of it de-pends upon our interpretation. And what can be interpreted can be re-interpreted.

There are some things about yourself that you cannot change; for instance, your history. At birth, you are thrown into a set of circum-stances and conditions about which you had no say, and which, to a tremendous degree, determine who you will be as you grow up. You have no choice in the matter. Much of your life is chosen by the circumstances and conditions of your personal and cultural history. Those circumstances and conditions, which include language, religion, nationality, ethnicity, gender, chronology, parents, and socioeco-nomic conditions, represent the skeleton of your structure of interpre-tation which you then flesh out with your own experiences throughout life. Given the particular skeleton you were "thrown" to, you are somewhat limited in terms of the possible musculature that you can develop.

You can only interpret yourself given the state of affairs you were thrown into at birth. You cannot change the facts. But you can shift the significance of the facts in how you interpret them. The facts of your history, culture, race, religion, gender, economy, and so on, determine the possible interpretations available to you. How you in-tegrate those facts into your identity, whether they limit or empower you, is within your control. To give you an example, maleness and femaleness are objective facts. But masculinity and femininity are cultural interpretations. In the United States of the 1950s tenderness and sensitivity were generally rejected as masculine traits. In the 1980s, however, they are accepted and even welcome qualities in "real men." And the American evaluations of masculinity may not match those of the Burmese during the same period. And, by the year 2000, American opinion about masculinity may radically change once again. The same can be said of feminine qualities. Thus, our interpretations are rooted in our specific, already existing environment.

Your already given interpretations provide the canvas upon which you paint your picture of the world. Each stroke you make, each color choice, each pattern, becomes part of your overall identity, and forms the basis for subsequent actions and decisions. Given the palette and brushes assigned to you at birth, you proceed to clarify and manifest your values and your commitments throughout your life.

Our morals and values are intimately connected with our personal interpretations. Your self-interpretations influence your value system, the system by which you distinguish between what is important and what is not, what is right or wrong, good or bad. They also influence your experience of the events in your life. For instance, the same mistake made by a Westerner may be experienced in a dramatically different way than if made by a Japanese. For the Westerner, it may be an embarrassment, whereas the Japanese may "lose face" completely. Based on different structures of interpretations, the same event could be experienced as survivable humiliation for a Westerner, and as an unpardonable loss of honor for the Japanese.

While you cannot change the facts of your history, you can shift your interpretation of those facts. It is as much a part of being human to be a product of your personal and cultural history as it is to be a product of your *interpretation* of your personal and cultural history.

ANOTHER INTERPRETATION OF THE SELF

If you believe that human beings are fixed, concrete, self-actualizing entities, then transformation is a theoretical contradiction. If you are immutable at your core, you cannot transform. If you hold human beings, rather, as collections of relationships, actions, interpretations, and concerns, then transformation is possible. Which theory is accurate is one of those questions that will probably never be answered definitively. There is no "Truth" and debating that issue will not further the work at hand. Lifespring's technology is designed on the philosophical premise that human beings are *not* fixed, atomic, objective, quantifiable beings. Rather, as the existential philosophers (including Søren Kierkegaard, Martin Heidegger, Maurice Merleau-Ponty, and Friedrich Nietzsche) have suggested, human beings are defined by self-interpretations that are determined primarily by the conditions of a specific time and place in history. There is voluminous work in philosophy and the social sciences that credibly challenges the fixed self view of human being. While it is a fascinating inquiry, it is not the purpose of our work together, and so I will close with the question: Are you certain that you are a fixed, concrete, atomic self with fixed, inevitable traits? If so, are you certain enough to forfeit the possibilities available in exploring a nonfixed interpretation of the self? Consider this alternative philosophical interpretation of the self.

There are no fixed, concrete components in us; human beings are interpretations all the way down. If you take away interpretation, you are merely left with a pile of flesh and bones. What makes us "who we are" as distinct from other things, including other living things, is our self-interpreting nature. Our reality consists of our interpretations—if you will, how we digest, process, and integrate our perceptions, and the significance we assign to what happens in our lives. Unlike things, which have some objective qualities that cannot be altered without changing the very nature of the things themselves, fundamental shifts can and do occur in human beings that yet embrace and preserve the consistency of their being.

Let's explore the roots of the proposition that the self is a product of interpretation.

In our culture, people's images and self-characterizations are predominately seen as rigidly fixed qualities. In other words, people think certain ways of being are "just the way they are." But is this a fact? In order to say that "I am shy," "I am passive," or "I am aggressive," logic would have it that there must be something concrete within you that has those characteristics. If this is true, then where is it? In your soul? Your mind? Your personality? Your body? Could we cut you open and see it? Further, it requires that you have the ability to evaluate yourself objectively. But how can you be sure that you have separated the objective facts about yourself from your feelings, prejudices, opinions, preferences, and biases? You cannot separate "factual" reality from your interpretation of it. The "fixed self" theory is just an assertion; the one that happens to be the prevalent point of view in our culture, but not one that has a factual basis.

If the idea of a concrete self within us isn't "the Truth," then why is it the cultural point of view, and why do we all accept it so automatically? If our characterizations are merely products of our interpretations, why do we cling to them so strongly even when they don't work? What is the significance to us if this fixed view of human nature is not correct, but merely an interpretation?

Indeed, there is a tremendous store of evidence to support the fixed self concept. First, and most obviously, there is your body. Sure, your body changes throughout your life, and you have some control over your shape, size, and appearance. But basically, you don't get much of a vote about your body. You're stuck with the physical features you have thanks to your genes. The body you do have absolutely limits your possibilities—if you are born male, you don't have a choice about bearing children. But your physical features are just that: your physical features. The only effect they have on your experience of life is that they color how you see the world, your *interpretation* of what it is to be human. For instance, your physical body determines whether you interpret from the stance of a male or female, tall person or short person, and so on. Second, our language reinforces the fixed self concept and supports us to interpret ourselves as fixed. In our communication with each other, we make distinctions like "I," "you," and "it." Who said those distinctions are correct? Could "I" exist without "you?" They are not separate phenomena, but we live within language that creates a separation. If there is a distinct "I," then it must have distinct characteristics. We *do* each have distinct characteristics, but our language does not discern between those that are fixed—like height, eye color, and gender—and those that are merely interpretation—like shyness, assertiveness, beauty, and intelligence. We think our language was invented to describe or represent reality, but language and reality are intertwined—language not only shapes our *interpretation* of reality, but shapes how reality itself unfolds. Our language is so central to who we are and how we think that it is difficult to even imagine an interpretation that doesn't fit the structure of language. Third, as mentioned before, the history into which we are thrown at birth is a fixed framework of unchangeable facts. It cannot be "transformed." So, part of the human condition is, by nature, uncontrollable and predetermined. What we can do, though, is transform how we deal with what can't change. At an essential level, the self is constructed by a tapestry of interpretations. Anything about us that is fixed is indivisible from our interpretation of it and our interrelations with the rest of the world.

Which point of view provides more of an opening for transformation? My claim should be obvious by now. It may surprise you to know that Lifespring's philosophy has changed over the last two decades. In the Basic Training, we used to talk about the "diamond within" each of us, a metaphor that alluded to a perfect, natural self within. We encouraged people to strip away the beliefs, memories, and hurts that were blocking the natural expression of their "real" inner selves. Over the last several years, out of our commitment to question and entertain new possibilities, as an organization we have shifted. We questioned our philosophical foundation and discovered that it wasn't solid, nor was it the most empowering way to work with people. We were asking people to express their "true selves," as though we knew what a true self was, as though it were a tangible organ like your heart or lungs. Out of our continual inquiry we have come to hold human beings as possibilities, limited only by our interpretations of them, and by the history, language, and commitments in which we live. This current understanding of human nature may not be the truth, the light, and the way, but it stands up to rigorous analysis, and more effectively opens you up to taking action to discover new possibilities for your future.

You may ask, if there is nothing fixed and definite about human beings, then how do we get our identities; what determines our personalities; what causes each of us to have unique style, tastes, and preferences; what makes us who we are? Great questions!

SELF-INTERPRETATION

What makes us who we are, what determines our every word and action, is our interpretation of ourselves and the world in relationship to ourselves. This is a tough idea to articulate. For the sake of illustration, here is a simple example:

1. Something happens; for instance, you get invited to a high-level business conference.
2. You have some thoughts and feelings about that; for instance, you feel proud or you are surprised that you were included.
3. You interpret your thoughts and feelings, either consciously or uncon-

sciously; for instance, 'I am good at what I do,' or 'I'm not really as good as they must think I am.'

4. That interpretation becomes part of the road map of your identity; for instance, you are successful, or, you are a fraud.

Here's another example:

1. Something happens; for example, as a kid, you fall down right in the middle of the classroom and the other kids laugh.
2. You have some thoughts and feelings about that; for instance, you are embarrassed, you start crying, you are mad at yourself, you feel like an idiot, you fear that your friends won't like you anymore.
3. You interpret your thoughts and feelings, either consciously or unconsciously; for instance, 'I have to look good all the time if I want people to like me.' 'If I don't have everything under control, I'll humiliate myself.'
4. That interpretation becomes part of the road map of your identity; for instance, your priorities become looking good, being in control, and never letting others see you unguarded.

Such interpretations as "I am successful," or "I have to be in control" are thus invented by you, but you don't have much of a choice about them. You respond to events in specific ways because of your history and physical reality.

Consider here the possibility that, since your identity has emerged out of your interpretations, you may be able to reinvent yourself. Use the following suggestions to direct your inquiry.

• Think back through your past. Identify some significant events that helped shape the road map of your identity. What happened? What thoughts and feelings did you have? How did you interpret those thoughts and feelings? In what ways are you still acting out of those interpretations?
• What difference would being able to reinterpret yourself make in your life?

For those of you who are skeptics, I can hear your wheels turning now. You are thinking: "Okay, so I am nothing but a bunch of interpretations. Then what generates those interpretations? Who's behind the wizard's curtain? Are you saying that there are no objective facts?

Do you mean that if I accept this point of view, I am free to pick a new identity off the interpretation rack at the grocery store? And what about these unlimited possibilities? So I can blink my eyes and create the identity of neurosurgeon when I have been a diesel mechanic all my life?" No, controlling your interpretations is not wizardry, and you cannot just wave your magic wand and pick the interpretation, "I am a black woman," if what you are is a white man. There are boundaries that limit the possibile interpretations to which you have access.

Within the limitations of aspects of our physical existence and our history, however, you have the power to redeclare the context of your interpretations. Hence, life is a dance of continual invention. Conversely, in the fixed self model you are merely playing out a course that is governed by allegedly fixed qualities you were allotted at birth. Compare the freedom of designing yourself out of the background of your history and your physical constraints to the inevitability of a life predetermined by your history and physical constraints.

In the fixed self understanding, your interpretations are perceived as facts—like verdicts. If you hold that people are who and what you interpret them to be, however, then you are likely to approach yourself and others as possibilities, and you are likely to find openings rather than closures. You are more likely to look for unexpected genius from yourself and others rather than to plug people into fixed and limiting categories.

This interpretation of human beings—that we *are* what we interpret, and that there is nothing intrinsically fixed about us other than that we are temporal beings—is a suggestion, an hypothesis. Think of this view, not as the enlightened truth about life, but as an effective way by which to enter into communication with the world.

Answer the following questions in your journal to begin the exploration of yourself as interpretation:

- What fixed qualities have you ascribed to yourself?
- How does that characterization dictate your actions? How do your actions, in turn, validate your characterization?
- Think of two or three people close to you. What fixed qualities have you ascribed to them?
- How do your characterizations of people around you limit what could be possible?
- Consider that you can change your interpretations, without any evidence, just because you say so. Write down your thoughts.

Dave and Joan Zoller

7

GRADUATE PROFILE

Dave and Joan Zoller, married twenty-eight
years, and in their fifties, were so moved by their
Lifespring trainings that they took on the extraordinary task of bringing the trainings back to
their friends and family in Kansas City.

"I remember thinking one night," says Joan,
"that I had had a great day, but I had no feeling
of passion about anything. I remember thinking
I would love to feel passionate about something
in my life, to have a life's work, something that
would carry me on through the rest of my life.
I felt like an unfinished woman. I had been a
housewife and raised kids, and felt that there was
something else ahead of me. I had to make a

decision about what I wanted to do with the rest of my life. I had another life coming and didn't know what it was about. I had a great relationship with Dave. We had just built our dream house on thirty acres. We had raised five great kids and had several beautiful grandchildren. Since the kids have grown, we've done whatever we've wanted to do. Dave makes a good living. I have felt no material limitations. I've had everything in the world I could ever want. Yet, sitting in my beautiful home doing decorating and gardening would just be maintenance, hanging on to what I had, playing it safe. I didn't understand my lack of passion in the midst of abundance.

"I think the Basic Training is wonderful for everybody," continues Joan, "but I think it's especially important for people who are in mid-life. At this point in our lives, having been married twenty-eight years and raised our family, we've done what we set out in our lives to do. So where do we go from here? The attitudes of society have changed so much: toward women, toward aging. It used to be that people our age were settling down to enjoy their golden years for ten more years before they died. That's not true anymore. And yet people our age are frequently still operating on old principles of stereotypical roles for the ideal woman and the ideal man. It's especially important to step outside those roles and be willing to take a look at our lives and to recognize that society is changing and that we are really in a position to push against some of the barriers that society has set up. By living what I got out of the Basic, I am making my life really exciting instead of being old ahead of my time."

Dave, formerly a pathologist, has begun a new chapter in his life by leaving his thirty-year profession to manage the Lifespring center in Kansas City. "When I was twelve years old, my dream was to take care of people and assist people in making their lives work. That's why I went into pathology. I admittedly had fears about leaving that to become a manager for Lifespring because I had doubts about whether I could do the job. Pathology is like falling off a log for me. I know the work from A to Z. It doesn't threaten me at all. My services are always in demand, I get well paid for those services, and I have a comfortable living as a result. In the Basic Training I discovered that there are ways I can contribute to people that I had never thought about before. All of a sudden I was looking at making this jump to doing something I'm not trained for. I really struggled with the decision. On the one hand, I didn't know if I'd succeed. Yet on the other hand, I didn't want to look back on this opportunity and wonder why I never did what I wanted to do.

"Once I made the choice it was really easy, even though I had been way out of my comfort zone during the time leading up to the decision. Once I made the leap, there was no resistance, it just created a new, broader comfort zone. It's exciting for me because I keep mastering my life by going up against bigger challenges. I feel I have put that twelve-year-old's dreams into action."

How did it all begin for Dave and Joan? First, Dave's brother took the Basic Training, then their son, and then one of their daughters. In one of many conversations about it, their daughter told Joan that it was the most liberating experience she had ever had. "That spoke to both of us," says Dave. "Maybe there was something to it. I still had this judgment that there's nothing of any real lasting value there, but I was ready to give it a try.

"When we got to Denver and went into the training, I knew I was going to participate fully even though I didn't know why the hell I had decided to come. The first night I argued with the trainer for about forty-five minutes about coming back from Kansas City a week later for the Post Training, which I had no intention of doing. I was ready to leave at the break."

During this time, Joan was pulling on Dave's coattails. "I wanted him to just sit down. Tell them you'll be there and then don't show up. I didn't stand up because there was no reason why I couldn't come back. But I was really angry. I thought the trainer was the most arrogant son of a bitch I had ever seen in my life."

"I wasn't going to sit down," continues Dave. "Either I would stay and be in agreement with the Ground Rules, or not. In retrospect, I actually think I was trying to manipulate a situation where I would get thrown out of the training and I wouldn't have to do it. I decided to stay. Throughout the training whenever there was sharing my hand went up. I must have talked every day at least two or three times. I just started pouring myself out and I really began to get an experience of the love I have for people."

"And the more this happened with him," Joan interjects, "the more backed up I got. By Friday I had one of my major migraines. I was very sick. This was my avoidance. I wasn't going back Friday night. I didn't see how I could possibly sit there and be this way. I knew inside that something was happening for me, but I didn't understand it. And seeing Dave so involved scared me to death. I was scared I was going to be left behind."

Joan did go back, and Friday night something opened up individually for both of the Zollers during one of the exercises. "I realized how much of my life I let go by without standing up and making myself heard," Joan recalls. "Without taking a stand. Even if I knew what was right and how to do something, I would make an attempt, but would back down at the first little puff of wind that came my way. When the trainer explained the rules of the game we were to play, I understood and knew what to do right away. I stood up and told my team how to win the game. They told me to sit down, that I didn't know what I was talking about. I angrily went to the back of the room, folded my arms and sat there saying to myself, 'Okay, don't listen to me. Go ahead and lose. Then I can say I told you so.' When we finished the game and looked back at our own participation, I was heartsick because I realized what I had done. I had let someone else take the responsibility, and the game was lost. I hadn't put myself on the line. It was a real eye-opener for the rest of my life in that I recognized how I was hiding out everywhere, playing it safe. I had built this nest around myself. I thought it was going to be safe, but I was closing down within it. Saturday morning I was one of the first ones to stand on the stage and share. I was scared to death. When I walked off that stage, I knew that I had to deal with a lot of those things in my life that I now had new insight into. I couldn't go backwards."

Meanwhile, Dave, who was on the other team in the game, was also facing, among other things, his reluctance to take a stand. "There was a woman sitting next to me. She was very soft-spoken. We were discussing the game and she explained to me how to win. I stood up and said that she had something to say and I wanted everyone to listen. She wouldn't get up and speak, so I told them what she had explained to me. I put it out, but wouldn't take a real firm stand about it. If they were not going to listen to it, they were not going to listen to it. Obviously, they didn't.

"Some guy had jumped up to be the captain of our team. How I played the game after not being listened to was to criticize his participation. He was totally out of control. Who appointed this jerk captain anyway? What was significant was that I did not get up and be the captain of the team and run it the way it needed to be run. I didn't take a stand.

"What was really disturbing was how blind I was to the purpose of the game. I was so focused on my own competitive drive, that I didn't even see the possibility that the game was really trying to demonstrate. I didn't even listen to the instructions, I was so busy calculating how to win the competition, how to beat the other team."

After having really engaged in the training process, Joan continued to have breakthroughs. "During another exercise, we were imagining ourselves sailing our own boats. That was truly my turning point. I had been a housewife, Mrs. Nice Guy, all my life, and hadn't worked since we married. Over the years we had sailed some, but I was always too scared to ever be on my own on the boat. In the closed eye exercise in the Basic, though, I was enjoying this incredible feeling of being in charge of this beautiful, shiny craft. In the picture in my mind, I looked over to the side and saw Dave in his boat. He waved and I waved back. Then I looked to the other side and there were all five of my children in their own boats. We were all going along in a line together, but we were each in our own boat. I didn't think ahead on this, it just happened spontaneously in my imagination. Instantly I realized that I could be out there in the world on my own, that I didn't need to depend on Dave for who I was or what I was doing. And I didn't need to depend on my image of being a mom and a granny. They all have their own lives to go forward with and I am free to go forward with mine.

"It's funny because on the way out of the room for the break after that exercise, someone turned to me and said that it was the dumbest thing they had ever experienced and a total waste of time. I wondered how they could say that. My whole life had changed and I was walking about a foot off the ground! One result of that experience is that the next fall I enrolled in school. I had gone back to college years before, but stopped. I kept saying I'd go back someday—as soon as the house is finished, as soon as so-and-so has her baby. I've been going ever since and have one more year to complete my degree."

Dave remarks on another significant experience: "During the whole training I remember sitting in the room looking up at this silly sign that said, 'What Are You Pretending Not To Know?' Seeing that sign every day irritated me so much. I did not generally spend a lot of time in introspection. I kept thinking there's nothing I'm pretending not to know. I know everything about myself. Maybe they're talking to somebody else. Finally, actually months later, I began to acknowledge how much I don't know and that there is a ton I am pretending not to know. I'm still just beginning to open up to some of those things; the process just keeps unfolding and unfolding. There was a little peephole in the Basic that keeps getting bigger and bigger and bigger."

How has doing the training changed the Zollers' lives?

Dave: "It has created a tremendously free space to operate from. My appreciation of Joan just grows daily. Often when Joan would speak to me in the old days, my internal conversations with myself were so loud I never even heard her. Whenever she addressed me, what was going on in my head was, 'She doesn't know what she's talking about.' That has stopped. Now I recognize that she did know what she was talking about. It was me who didn't know what I was talking about a lot of the time. I recognize that she's got a point of view and, while it may not be in total agreement with my point of view, it's valuable nevertheless, and it's something for me to look at. And so what's happened is I've become more vulnerable and much less defensive about protecting myself. It's opened me up to a relationship with Joan that is free of control. I don't have to control. She doesn't have to control. The power that gets generated from that is fantastic.

"During and after the training, little things kept coming up. All the garbage of twenty-eight years of marriage that had been swept under the rug. We each knew each other's spots not to touch if we wanted to keep peace. My way of dealing with those things previously was to just sweep them under the rug rather than be honest and open and confront the issue. All that began to come back out again. Once we got all that out and sorted it out and dealt with it, it all disappeared."

Joan: "It took a period of time for us to do that. Now that we've done that, it's changed our whole relationship. On my part, there's a tremendous feeling of admiration and tenderness and caring for Dave. We both experience the success of having a new life together. And it's a partnership in the best sense of the word because we're working together to focus *out* in our lives instead of getting something from each other. We do get something from each other, but our relationship isn't about what I'm going to get from him or what he's going to get from me. That has made possible some decisions and choices that weren't possible before. He has made tremendous space for me to put myself forward as a person, as a woman. In return, I want to allow him the space to do what he wants to do in his life. He's supported me and our children materially for thirty years. I want to pitch in and be productive so that I can give him the freedom to do exactly what he wants to do. I have a great feeling about it because I'm furthering myself by getting out in the world and contributing something here to our mutual support.

"Dave leaving his practice and going to work for Lifespring was a tremendous exercise for me in letting go of my need for security. He made a good living. But I feel like we're ready to move on. I've found that I don't want *things* anymore. What is most important to me doesn't have a dollar sign value. This change has given me the opportunity to put my money where my mouth is. I look at it as a challenge.

"This is another chapter. After the training, I have never since had that experience of feeling unfinished. I've got commitments to complete yet, but I still feel total. The passion is there. And this is a passion that we share. Hand in hand we're leaping ahead. And that, to me, is really exciting."

Image

8

PRIVATE CONVERSATIONS

Personal breakthrough requires that you give up certain beliefs about the way you, the world, and others are. Your interpretations determine how the world shows up for you. In other words, your beliefs dictate what you see and how you see it. For illustration, have you ever heard someone else describe an event that you also attended, but their memory of it is very different from yours? The things that stood out for you about the event weren't even mentioned by that person, and/or the things he or she remembered as important were far less significant in your memory. The source of this discrepancy is that you both have different structures of interpretation through which you process facts. Your *private conversations,* the conversations you have with yourself as you are sorting and interpreting the world, are different from other peoples'. Your private conversation is that conversation you have with yourself that you do not reveal to others, the thoughts, comments, and opinions that may not be secrets, but that you keep to yourself. We all have unique private conversations based on our different histories, cultures, and individual experiences. Thus, the distinctions each of us makes about what is important and what is unimportant are different from other peoples'.

PUBLIC CONVERSATIONS

Further, to have breakthrough in your life you will definitely be challenging and shifting your public conversations. *Public conversation,* in this usage, doesn't just mean the verbal exchanges you have with others. Rather, it means the totality of your external interactions with people and your environment. In the training we call it your "image." Your image is the persona you project, the "you" that others see and that is designed to conceal portions of your private conversation that are inconsistent with that persona.

THE IMAGE

Consider this example. You are invited to a party. Like everyone invited to that party, you spend all afternoon getting ready. Or, rather, you're getting your image ready. You put on the clothes that convey the message you want to convey (casual, formal, yuppie, artsy, sexy, athletic, funky, professional, etc.). Perfect hair to suit the outfit. Makeup for women. Maybe you practice a few smiles in the mirror. And, as long as you are in front of the mirror, maybe you dance around a little to make sure you still have the moves. You look hot. When you arrive at the party, what do you do? You look around for the people whose images are attractive to you and who you guess will be attracted to yours. Then you see him or her. Across the room. Looking hot. When his or her eyes, also scanning the crowd, meet yours, what do you do? You look away. Maybe at some point your images meet each other. If they do, your images exchange a few pleasantries. The next day, you call your friend and get this person's phone number. A few more days go by before it's cool to call. Your heart is pounding as you begin. "Hi, you may not remember me, but we met at the party last Saturday." Having been imagining what to say to you since the night of the party, his or her heart is also pounding as he or she responds. "Well, I'm not sure if I remember. Let me think." Then there is a grueling moment of silence. "Oh yes! Are you the one who was wearing the . . . ?" So your images have their first telephone conversation and set up a date for the following weekend. Who shows up for the date? Of course, your image shows up to check it out. And, of course, so does your date's image. You've both spent all day shining your images. You've washed your image car, gotten a manicure, and bought new clothes. You eat at a suitably image-y restaurant. You have the perfect image music in your tape deck, cued-up so the perfect image song comes on, "coincidentally," at the perfect moment on the way home. The next day you either send or receive the dozen red image roses with the clever image notecard. Et cetera, et cetera, et cetera.

Is it possible to continue this image courtship, proceed into an image marriage and be in that image relationship for five years, ten years, or more, and never have really "shown up"? Not only is it possible, but likely, considering that most of us can't distinguish between our images and what we really stand for as human beings. Your image is about survival and safety, not about passion and authenticity. In fact, it is determined to extinguish passion and authenticity because they might damage the image's strategy.

Our culture is set up so that we encourage each other's images and are relatively unaware of it. We are immersed in our inauthenticity. It's a social conspiracy where if you buy mine, I'll buy yours.

While your "style" is a valuable mechanism for expressing what is important to you and for connecting with people, maintaining and getting lost in a fixed self-image can mask what is really important to you and keep you detached from others at an essential level. Your *style*, meaning the distinct manner or tone you assume, is flexible according to the circumstances and to your standards. The problem with a fixed self-image or character is that it becomes an automatic mechanism that dictates how you participate in the world the majority of the time.

Why do we develop these images? Images are protective shields. Through our images, we support an illusion that we have some control over our acceptance and approval by others. What image do you project to guarantee approval of others: the professional, the nurturer, the happy and/or nice person, the intellectual, the macho man, the unique individual, Mr. or Ms. Cool, the efficient hard worker . . . ? Again, the danger isn't in having an image, it is in being totally absorbed in your image and allowing your actions to be narrowly contained within the boundaries of that image. Ultimately, your image is an insurance policy for your ego. If something doesn't turn out the way you wanted it to, you can rationalize it. For instance, it wasn't really that she didn't want to hire you, it was that you are just too "X" —or not "X" enough—to work in that position. Hence, you separate and insulate yourself from hurt, rejection, failure.

Another way to illuminate your image is to look at your need to *look good*. This concern is a natural part of human beings, it is there for all of us. Look at a typical example of how you are run by your need to look good. You are attracted to someone and would like to ask him or her for a date. But you don't. Why? Most of us say that fear of rejection keeps us from risking with other people. But the issue isn't really about having your invitation declined. You will not be irreparably damaged if you don't spend an evening with that person. The most dreaded part of being turned down isn't about not getting a date, it's embarrassment, losing face, not looking good—so, many times we don't ask at all. This is not only true about relationships. Have you ever tried to psych yourself up to ask for a raise, and then not asked? Have you ever tolerated a problem in your community because you didn't want to risk looking aggressive or foolish to your friends and neighbors? What becomes more important for us than the possibility of a new relationship, a raise, making a difference in our community, or whatever, is our need to look good at all costs.

Our need to be right and our fear of being dominated or controlled by others are also powerful motivators. Virtually all of our projects affect and are affected by other people. Ironically, however, we often shy away from asking for assistance, acknowledging another point of view, or reaching out to someone at the very times when it could make the crucial difference. We vigorously defend our beliefs, our opinions, and the validity of our actions and reactions, in order to be right and be in control. Even when we could further a project by stepping aside, by turning over the leadership role, or by asking for support, we're stuck in our egos. So often we would rather compromise our purpose than give in, admit we're wrong, let someone else be the star or ask for assistance.

What is the price we pay for operating out of our automatic images? Primarily, we are disconnected from people. We experience separateness. We forfeit intimacy, passion, and closeness because of our stubbornness and our illusions that we can keep from getting hurt.

In terms of causing the best possible results, living this way isn't very logical. Yet, it is true for all of us to different degrees. To deny that you ever operate this way will block possibilities for break-through.

Ironically, much of the effect of the "human potential movement" has been to allow people to "get in touch with who they really are," accept themselves, and make peace with themselves as they are. The value of that is significant, but the language used to articulate it is limiting. "Accepting yourself as you are" sounds like there is a concrete self somewhere within you that has an unchangeable character and must, therefore, be accepted as it is because it cannot shift under any circumstances. In the fine distinction between resigning yourself to a character which you have decided is true and real, and accepting the aspects of life which you can't change (your history, biological reality, and past choices, for instance), lies the possibility of transformation.

In the human potential school, your truly magnificent self has been obscured or handicapped during your past. "Human nature," they say, is essentially pure and good. Your job is to uncover the perfect gem within you and actualize its mighty potential. The work of transformation, conversely, doesn't rely on the notion of a perfect self within. Instead, transformation addresses questions like: What is possible for you in reinterpreting what it is to be a human being? What would it mean to you to have the freedom to re-invent your identity? If you could, in fact, design your behavior, how would you be different? Are you willing to pursue this possibility? If so, what actions do you promise to take to further that commitment, and who can assist you in the process?

There is definitely something mysterious about being human that cannot be described or defined, cannot be categorized as fixed or not fixed. Trusting in that brilliant mystery is uplifting and calming, while submitting to the confines of an unchangeable self can cause a sense of helplessness and anxiety.

How many times have you said something like, "I am a shy person," "If only I were more assertive," "People are always ignoring me," "I am boring," "I'm bad with numbers," "I am not athletic," "It's a rat race," "I couldn't use a computer if my life depended on it," and so forth. It is easy to see the limitations caused by such evaluations.

Even the stories we tell about ourselves that sound positive are limiting. "I am good in business," "I am happiest out-of-doors," "I am a nice person," "My strength is my logical mind," "My strength is my caring heart," and so on. Whether you assess your character traits as positive or negative is irrelevant to this discussion. The important question is: What possibilities do your characterizations of yourself and the world inherently close?

Hiding behind an image, looking good, being right, and avoiding domination, are several of the reasons why human beings stifle their natural and authentic self-expression. The key distinction to make for yourself is to determine whether your current practices and self-characterizations further you or inhibit you. In those cases where they inhibit you, you probably find the most tension and stress in your life. Honest inquiry into your image is a place to start the process of redesigning yourself for effective action.

Answer the following questions in your journal:

- How would you describe your image?
- How do you behave when you are trying to look good, be right, or avoid domination?
- How do these behavior patterns get in the way of accomplishing what you say you want?
- How do these behavior patterns affect your relationships with others?

THE RISK OF BEING AUTHENTIC

Your image may temporarily keep you less vulnerable to being hurt, but ultimately it closes down possibilities available to you. In contrast, authenticity and openness allow for breakthrough. Do you ever think about your patterns? Patterns in relationships, in jobs, in physical well-being, in finances, and so on? Who said life adheres to patterns? Who said you can't interrupt a pattern and shift out of it? You can, but only if you are willing and, in fact, committed to breaking up your image.

Breakthrough occurs through *inventing* your identity from nothing, not through improving your already entrenched image; it requires a willingness to forfeit the predictable future that your image ensures. Inventing your identity, as distinct from setting goals, demands that you behave in new and unfamiliar ways. It is a risky endeavor. Your image is comfortable and it probably works in many ways or you wouldn't have developed and nurtured it. To access possibilities that exist *outside* your image, you must risk the unknown. You cannot attend a preview, check it out, and then decide if you are going to stick with your image or go for the breakthrough. There is no guarantee about where the process will take you. It will be a struggle because your image's whole reason for existing is to keep you invulnerable, and your image has a fierce will to survive intact.

It is in the process of questioning yourself and challenging your fixed notions that breakthrough occurs. If, after any process, you are still singing the same old song, you have not been willing to integrate the new information in a way that makes a positive difference for yourself and the world. The operative word here is *difference,* implying that there is something missing in the status quo. It takes vulnerability and humility to admit that something is missing about you, far too much vulnerability for many people, given the gigantic attachment they have to looking good.

I have searched for years for a way to be committed, authentic, involved with people, and yet remain invulnerable. Similarly, I have searched for a way to accomplish breakthrough without risking the security of my image. I haven't found either.

In your journal, answer the following questions about your image:

- What image do you project at work?
- What image do you project at home?
- What image do you project in social situations?
- How does your image protect you? From what does it protect you?
- What rewards do you gain by acting out of that image?
- What price do you pay?
- What price might you pay if you gave up that image?
- What rewards might you gain?

Gene Ciancio and Lisa Hoffman-Ciancio

9

GRADUATE PROFILE

Gene Ciancio, an attorney and municipal court judge in Colorado, originally did the Basic Training in order to fix his wife, Lisa. "I thought it was a brilliant plan," recalls Gene. "I really was anticipating that I could get her fixed."

At first, Lisa, who had recently suffered the loss of her hair from an illness called alopecia areata, was completely closed to doing the training for several reasons. For one thing, she sensed Gene's motives, and "I was more or less against anything Gene had to offer at that point. Also, given how I was raised, I was not open to anything in the self-awareness realm. My family just thought those things were ridiculous. So I automatically said 'It won't work and I'm not going.' Plus, I had just lost all of my hair because of alopecia. I knew that someone would want to hug me and my wig would fall off. I had not really dealt with the hair loss yet. I was in a major depression about it. I thought this training would be too confrontive. I was a professional victim. I wasn't open at all to the idea that you could possibly be responsible for your life."

"We had gone to a marriage counselor after we started living together," Gene explains, "because right on top of our brand new relationship entered my fourteen-year-old daughter who moved in with us. I was thirty-five, Lisa was twenty-five, and Cindy was fourteen—all in the same household. We decided early on that if we were ever going to make our relationship work we had to get some assistance with how to communicate around the issues, mainly about Cindy."

"Our marriage was really at a turning point," continues Lisa. "We knew that we either had to do something fast or it wasn't going to last. I knew in my heart that something had to change. And it was me, not Gene. No one else in my life could be responsible for me. I was seeing a great therapist about the alopecia. But that psychological path was really about delving into the past and telling stories about my life and talking about my parents; there was some movement there, but it wasn't really supporting me in taking responsibility for my own life. I knew that I had to make some changes. I knew that I had wallowed in self-pity about losing all my hair for long enough.

"I didn't want to go to the Guest Event with Gene, but I basically had to. We have this numbering system where you assign a number between one and ten for how important something is to you. If it is below a five, the other person has the option to decline. But if it is a five or higher, it's pretty much hands down, you do it. You have to be honest about it. You can't say six if it's really only a three. So I asked Gene what number this Guest Event was and he said it was about a nine. So I went.

"As soon as we got to the Guest Event, and I heard the speaker, I knew I was going to do the training. I was back at the table signing up at the first chance, I think even before Gene."

"We both signed up," Gene said, "and that night, we had one of the worst fights we had ever had. Everything just started flushing up."

Lisa and Gene started the Basic Training about a week later. Lisa was immediately moved. "It was an amazing training for me. I had the best time I think I've ever had in my life. My life changed the first night. It was the little push I needed to move off of self-pity and look at where I was going. Thursday night I realized I had spent my whole life depressed and neurotic and guilty.

"I had no direction in life. I was bored in my paralegal position, I hated being a stepmother, our marriage was rocky, I had lost all my hair. My biggest goal was to acknowledge to myself and others that I was bald now. I didn't have my looks to hang onto, and knew that I might have to use my vulnerability in the world.

"During one exercise on Saturday morning, I told my partner that all I really wanted was to take my wig off. She's one of my best friends now, but not knowing about the alopecia at the time she thought I was crazy. She said 'You want to *what?*' I told her the story really fast, and she said 'So, take it off.' So, I did. I looked around. She wasn't throwing up, nobody around me was going into convulsions. I felt pretty comfortable. Then we put the chairs back in theater style and the trainer asked if anyone had anything to share. Well, I was pretty bashful, but I raised my hand. I said that for the first time I had dealt with my disease of hair loss. The whole experience had such a cleansing impact on me, I will never forget it. Since then, I have gone out in public bald.

"It turned my whole life around. Now I am an alopecia support group leader in Colorado, and a National Board member. All because I did the training. I've found major direction in my life with alopecia. I've personally helped hundreds of people."

Gene, meanwhile, remembers that "I was analytical through the Basic. I figured that this would be fine for most people, and I was glad that Lisa was getting fixed. For the most part, I was pretty much the observer, the supportive husband. I was being honest in small groups, but I was still pretty reserved. I was just there to help Lisa get fixed. I had heard almost everything in the Basic in other contexts. There wasn't anything in there that came as a total shock to me—responsibility and all that. I had literally read fifty books about that sort of philosophy; none of it was totally foreign to me intellectually. But the experiential parts of the trainings were great. That is where I really got most value. I saw how I was not using my talents and education. I was wimping out."

What was different about Lisa and Gene after they did the trainings? They agree that it's probably easier for them to describe the dramatic changes in each other than in themselves. "Gene," Lisa begins, "*showed up*. He's always been a wonderfully compassionate teddy bear, but after he did the training, I started seeing joy. Before the training, it was not uncommon to have an hour-long conversation with Gene and have his mind be on Mars for all but five minutes of it. That used to be my biggest complaint. His clients would say the same thing when I would deal with them between the time they met with Gene until their case went to trial. They would ask if something was wrong with him. He was so laid back, his business partners thought he was lazy. Other people just thought he was comatose. And all of a sudden, after the training, people were saying about Gene 'What a caring guy, I really get that he cares about me.'

"Now, Gene will say funny things from the bench. One guy called him a stupid son of a bitch and Gene looked down and said: 'If I'm so stupid, how come I'm going to Hawaii next week and you're going to jail?' He is really being innovative and making a big difference with people in his court. He has kids who have been habitual criminals since they were twelve. He has them write four or five pages about what they want out of life and out of their relationships with people. We get letters years later from people who Gene has sentenced saying what a difference that made for them. He asked one man when he was going to start loving himself. Gene talked with him about how that was stopping him and how his life would turn around when he started loving himself. Months later, that guy wrote us a letter saying: 'Thanks. You should be a judge the rest of your life. I stopped. I am responsible. I love myself now and I have a girlfriend. I have a car and a job as a dishwasher. And I am happy.' "

Gene says that what changed for him was that "I lightened up. I had been bored with everything. I woke up and came alive again. In the training they say life is not a dress rehearsal, but I had been living my life like that proverbial dress rehearsal. I really saw how much I sit back and criticize instead of being involved. That began a process for me of deciding to access my leadership abilities. The biggest turn for me was to realize that if you decide to be a leader and you're half-assed about it, that's the way the people you're leading will be. In that respect, I saw what I had created with the people in my law office, which wasn't much. I have come a long way in turning that around by caring about other people, serving people, and being responsible.

"Like I said, before the Basic I'd read a lot of the books and knew all of the jargon and the philosophies about responsibility and service and all that. The training gave me a language to translate that into words that I could really understand and put into action, and words that, in turn, I can communicate to others and have them understand. In my court we get a lot of small cases, shoplifting and stuff like that, so my court is the most likely place in the entire judicial system where the average person will see a judge. My purpose in being a judge is to translate a lot of those ideas about how to have life work to the public in a judicial form.

"After doing the training, I thought of this new procedure for a lot of kids I get in my court for shoplifting. The kids that come in front of me don't ever focus their attention outside themselves for even a fraction of a minute. They are self-centered literally all the time. Instead of just fining them and having them go to class, I've begun having them complete twenty hours of community service on their own. The key is that *they* have to go find a place to serve other people in the community. We used to have a program where we would have them go clean up the school or something, but they did it just because the court made them. Here, they have to go find it for themselves. One girl went to an animal shelter. Her mom's not too thrilled because she has brought home about five dogs, but when she came back to me after having completed her ten hours she was glowing. Her eyes were on fire. She said it was the most wonderful thing she had ever done, she loved it and was going to keep volunteering. Another guy came in with the same kind of spark in his eye. He had called the Head Start program in his county because he had read about it in the newspaper and asked if they had anything he could do. He was only fifteen and didn't think he could do anything for them. They told him to come on down, they had the perfect thing. They let him be the big brother to a four-year-old kid who had no brothers and sisters. That was it for this boy. Now, he takes this kid everywhere. Instead of going and hanging out around the drive-in or whatever he used to do, he's taking this little kid to the movies. His whole life has changed out of that. I rule that these kids have to spend ten or twenty hours in service, and they end up doing it for weeks or more. Three or four nonprofit agencies have written asking about the program, praising the kids. Creating this program comes directly out of what I personally picked up through Lifespring."

Now, here's what Gene has to say about Lisa: "The change in Lisa is phenomenal. When I met her, she was a paralegal. She used to take caffeine pills and other stimulants every morning to pump herself up in order to be able to type a thousand words a minute and make it through the day. That only accentuated her already energetic personality. At the end of the night, she'd be so wound up that it was like seeing somebody ready to explode. Plus, she was very involved with her physical problems; female things, headaches, backaches, knee problems. One of the things our relationship was based on in the beginning was her illnesses and my willingness to support her in them, getting her to the doctor, and so forth. Any mention by me that there could possibly be a mental component to her physical conditions was like asking to have my throat slit. The transformation in her life about feeling good and being ready to take on any project without having sickness be a concern is incredible. There is no question about it that the training is where that happened."

Lisa adds: "I got a lot of attention that way. Negative attention. I didn't understand it at the time, but I do now. I figured out in the training that whatever was going on with me was partly created by me. I fully take responsibility for my alopecia. It has given me a purpose in life. I had a nice, comfy job, and I was good at it, but so what? Where was I going? What was next for me? I know that this disease was brought into my life because (a) I needed to learn something very valuable, and, (b) I needed a purpose. I needed to be serving people. I think the alopecia happened to me because I have the ability to rise above it. My family has always been in shock of me and in awe of all of my 'drama,' but I have a survival kind of nature. I can handle this, and I can serve other people in learning how to deal with it.

"I took over the alopecia support group in Colorado and turned the whole thing around. The first meeting I went to had six people and was a doom and disaster convention. Everyone would tell their stories about how their lives had fallen apart since they got alopecia. 'What a tragedy, it's the worst thing that ever happened to me, I don't want to live, it's so sad.' And on and on. Now, I have sixty people attending meetings and 350 members. We talk about how to work with hair pieces and how to wear scarves. People walk out feeling good. We talk about the stages of loss—it's a lot like losing someone close to you. We make it okay for people to experience whatever stage they're in and then move on. Moving on is the key and it was totally missing from this group before I got there. All of a sudden my life has a purpose and I know that it's as a result of doing the training. Without the training, I never would have moved past my own self-pity."

What was it like for Gene to go through his wife's alopecia? "Here I am, somebody who married this beautiful young woman. Full of hair everywhere it was supposed to be. Blonde, of course. The lesson that came into my life through this was about what beauty really is. I went through exactly the same stages she went through. The problem was, we went through them at different times; there were times when she was in the stage of being angry when I was just depressed—and the last thing I wanted to see was some bald angry woman. There would be times when I was angry and she was in denial. I was pretty good at hiding it, but it was big for me. What I came out of it with was being totally committed to the relationship.

"Commitment is one of the things I learned the most about in the trainings. I had one particular experience that was probably the most important few minutes of my life as far as relationships. Lisa and I had stood up to share something about our relationship. We were complaining about something or other in our marriage. The trainer asked us to please go and find the place where it promises that you're going to be happy every minute in a relationship. It was no big deal and I'm sure some people were bored by the whole interaction, but it hit me hard. You mean we're not going to be happy all the time and our marriage can still work? From that day on we have had some royal battles, but there has never been one question in my mind about this commitment.

"We have both enrolled a lot of people in the training, but the best one was my daughter, Cindy. She had just turned eighteen when she did it. She has made such an incredible shift. Her life is just amazing. She was flunking school, skipping classes, smoking dope, wrecking cars. You name it, she did it. She used to climb out the window at night. When we first did the training and started talking to her about keeping her word she hated it. When she did the Basic Training, it was like night and day. She started at an alternative school and was the absolute head of the class in every respect; her attendance was excellent, she was getting good grades, and was being a leader with the other students. Now she's holding down a full-time job and going to school—and doing a great job in both."

Doing the trainings transformed the relationship between Lisa and Cindy. "We had been arch rivals, both vying for Gene's attention. Since doing the trainings, we have become best friends. She acknowledged that I was there supporting her and Gene, even when the going got tough. I recognized that a lot of the things about her I had trouble with were things I was desperately fighting against in myself. All three of us having done the trainings hasn't just transformed each of our individual lives, but has dramatically improved the quality of our family life together.''

Gene concludes: "Cindy pretty much sums it up for all of us. She got it loud and clear that she is responsible for her own life. She can't blame things on the world, on her parents' divorce, on her mean stepmother, or whatever. She got that it's up to *her* if she wants to be happy, and she did something about it.''

10

Intervention

An ancient Chinese proverb warns that if you don't change your direction, you are likely to end up where you are headed. Consider what the proverb implies—that you have some power to design or redesign your future.

I would say that, by and large, the human race is not heading in the direction that most of us envision in our dreams. Further, I am suggesting that each of us as an individual exists in an environment that does not support us in really being who we are. Quite the opposite—we live in a culture that supports us, even urges us, to conceal, stifle, and ridicule authentic expressions of our humanness.

A world that works for everyone is a culture

in which each of us is committed to each other's commitments. It is a global society in which sincerity, genuine support, and authenticity abound; where you are not afraid to really be who you are. This vision requires us to see past the ignorance, prejudice, and insensitivity of the status quo to a society that could be, but is not yet—a world where your contributions are amplified, not diminished. This vision is of an environment in which you are seen as a possibility and are supported in making a difference. This is a culture of courage and compassion where you and I can trust that we are here *for,* and not against, each other; where mistakes can be forgiven rather than merely seized upon to make others wrong. It is a society that values your well-being as more important than what you can be used for.

This society affords us the privilege and responsibility of both giving and receiving love, and joins individuality with interdependence in an empowering way. It allows each of us the honor of being personally charged with that responsibility in our lifetimes. This new culture lives today in our actions as well as in the future in our dreams. And each of us has the right to assume personal responsibility for it today. Right now.

I know that you have a vision. The practical tools offered to you here are intended to enable you to bring that vision closer to becoming a reality. Always remember to look forward to what it is you are working toward. Remember to look across the river first and remind yourself of your dreams. Then, look down at the river and figure out how to conquer the alligators that stand between you and your dreams.

INTERVENING

Imagine the power of being able to intervene between the present and the future in a way that shifts the seemingly automatic course you individually, and humankind collectively, are already on. In the domain of transformation, intervention is a commitment or act that shifts your practices in the present, thereby inventing anew how the future will unfold.

The circumstances of the past and present shape the possibilities for intervention. By your intervention, you generate a future that would not have occurred had you not interrupted the flow of events. Intervention is no magic wand and the possibility for intervention is shaped by the facts of reality. By intervening, you have an effect on how the future unfolds rather than drifting into the future that would inevitably follow the uninterrupted past. You can't intervene without facing up to what's happened in the past or is happening in the present. Intervention means participating in the present, in light of what has happened in the past, such that you generate and act on new possibilities for the future.

CONFORMITY AND THE DRIFT

Conformity is a fundamental, natural tendency of human beings. We all have a rock-bottom disposition to conform. You naturally adhere to the cultural norms into which you were born. Those cultural norms combine with your particular factual history (gender, nationality, age, and so on) to form a matrix of dispositions to behave "normally." That matrix determines your social roles as an individual and prescribes how you relate to others. People tend to cooperate, to act in ways that complement each others' roles and that consummate normal social relations. You don't have a choice about your baseline inclination to conform—that is a given human trait. Even "nonconformists" conform to social categories.

The problem is that the social norms and practices to which we conform don't necessarily serve us optimally. Socially, we react to peoples' behavior in ways that encourage imitation of "normal" practices and discourage deviation. Therefore, your possibilities as a particular individual are restricted. Most people (not you and me, of course, but *most* people) will tend to act like anyone else with a similar cultural background would in similar circumstances. Your choice is always to act as "anyone else" would in the same situation, or, to examine your concerns and act out of them—which may or may not mirror the cultural norm.

The cultural climate consists of the shared understandings and practices that form the backgrounds of our lives. Because of the apt imagery, this cultural backdrop has been called the "drift." For each of us the character of the drift differs depending on gender, age, race, religion, and so on. But the nature of the drift is the same for all human beings; it is inescapable, and to a great extent defines who you are and how you see the world. The drift limits your possibilities by predisposing you to interpret and act in accordance with the drift's interpretations and practices. As an American in the twentieth century, you cannot see and respond to the world the way an Englishman in the eighteenth century or an Egyptian in the twenty-first century would.

The drift is the cultural result of our tendency to conform. The drift is the trend, that which is already happening and from which the future can be predicted with a fair degree of accuracy. It denotes the path of least resistance. The drift is made up of our cultural norms. Our personal histories and our shared culture both shape and are shaped by the drift. What is appropriate and what is inappropriate are predetermined by the drift. Picture the drift as a rushing river that sweeps us along through our lives, predisposing us to act like anyone else. The drift isn't good or bad, it is just the current in which we float through life. The tendency to conform with the drift is in the nature of humanity.

Uninterrupted, the drift levels out the qualitative distinctions between what is important and what is unimportant. Acceptable human behavior is reduced to a narrow window of normalcy. Individuality is discouraged in the drift. Like a field leveled by a bulldozer for efficient construction, passion is flattened by the social drift of our culture to eliminate deviations in the human landscape.

The leveling effect of the drift suppresses actions that are extraordinary. Intervention allows the possibility of piercing the averageness that the drift generates. You can intervene in states of inevitability and resignation. Through your intervention, the future can be something other than merely a projection of the past. Your intervention can mean inventing the future rather than merely forecasting it. To return to our opening aphorism, intervention can enable you to shift the direction in which you are headed.

WHERE ARE YOU HEADED?

What's wrong with where you are headed? Nothing is necessarily wrong with it. Have you scrutinized where you are headed (meaning have you assessed the likely outcome of your current practices)? Have you honestly evaluated whether the path you are on today is likely to lead where you want to go, to the fulfillment of your life goals? Are your current behaviors consistent with your long-range commitments? Have you ever seriously examined and declared your life goals? (By goals, I do not mean specific achievements, necessarily. The word goal also refers to a general condition of satisfaction, commitment or end state.) What is your vision for your future? If you haven't declared your goals, what are they? Write them down in your journal.

WHAT INTERVENES?

What is the most effective vehicle for intervention? Commitment. A commitment, distinct from a hope, want, or intention, is demonstrated in your actions. It's what you are creating during the day, not what you dream about at night.

Look at a familiar example of how commitment is different from hope, wants, or intention. You declare that you are going to lose weight. You take on the exercise and dietary practices that will support your goal, but you don't lose weight, or you don't lose as much as you had intended to lose. If you're human, you've set goals like losing weight (or saving money, or calling your parents more frequently, etc.), and haven't accomplished those goals. Why not? The place to look is your practices. You did not *act* in a way that would achieve your goals. You may have sincerely wanted to lose weight, but based on the results, something else was more important. Your genuine commitment, as unlikely as it sounds, was to whatever end state you accomplished. Your commitment is to the actual end result that you are heading toward based on your *current* practices.

How can knowing this assist you except in retrospect? It's easy to see what you were committed to once you already have the result. Honing your ability to recognize *now* where your actions are leading you gives you the opportunity to intervene and alter the future outcome before it's too late. There is no power in waiting to get the result and *then* analyzing what you were really committed to. Who wants to be a reporter on his or her own life? There is also no power in just noticing what is happening while it's happening. Awareness is only as useful as the action it begets.

There is power in intervening when you find yourself in a breakdown so that you take action that directs you toward the accomplishment of your goal. The challenge of intervention is that it is impossible in hindsight. It requires you to shift your behavior now, in the face of the drift.

Consider these questions about your commitments, and take the opportunity to write your responses in your journal.

- Recall the life goals you declared in the last section. Based on your current practices, are they wants, hopes and intentions, or real commitments?
- What changes do you need to make in your behavior to be living in alignment with your commitments?

INTERVENTION IN ACTION

Intervention is a vehicle for breakthrough. One career in which we see people consistently intervening and triggering breakthrough is coaching. A coach's job is to intervene in the future. A coach intervenes and empowers committed students to shift their practices such that they become more competent, resolve breakdowns, open up new possibilities, and enhance their commitment.

What you are reading now is an example of intervention. This material is designed to interrupt the same old drift in which you *(we)* live. Ideally, you have experienced having your beliefs and behavior challenged, you have questioned the inevitability of your future, seen new possibilities for yourself, and been empowered to act on those possibilities. Why spend time and money to hear the same old rap, to fuel an engine that already has tremendous momentum? A key to your effectiveness will be your ability to *intervene* in the drift, to *interrupt* automatic behavior patterns that don't work, and *invent* new practices that do work.

For your further inquiry, consider the points and questions below. Write your responses in your journal.

- Identify some of the characteristics of the drift in which you live. Are some of them inconsistent with your life goals? Can you see any possibility for intervening in those?
- Has committing to this process (if you have) intervened in your behavior in any perceptible way yet? If not, I suggest that you are not committed to having this process make a difference in your life, that something else is more important to you.

CONVERSATIONS FOR INTERVENTION

Your commitment has the power to intervene and bring forth reality by both determining and being reflected in your actions. What's important to you will greatly determine what you do, and, in turn, what you do will greatly determine the evolution of what's important to you.

The type of action that most powerfully embodies and creates commitment is *speaking*. In your speaking you have the tools to intervene in any situation.

Certain communication does more than just represent reality, it actually brings forth reality. For instance, when you say "dog," a dog does not fall out of your mouth, but when you say "I promise," a promise does. When you say "marriage," a married couple doesn't pop out of your mouth. But, when someone with the appropriate qualifications says "I now pronounce you husband and wife," a new reality called marriage is created by virtue of that declaration. Certain types of conversation can intervene and create reality by bringing your commitments to life.

There are four types of conversation that intervene: promises, requests, declarations, and assertions. A brief definition of each follows:

PROMISE   To promise is to pledge yourself to do, bring about, or provide. A promise is a declaration to do or refrain from doing something specific. A promise creates an obligation. A complete promise requires: (1) a speaker, (2) a listener, (3) terms of fulfillment (exactly what will be produced), and (4) a time agreement.

REQUEST   Requesting is the act of asking for something from someone else. A complete request requires: (1) a speaker, (2) a listener, (3) terms of fulfillment (exactly what is being asked for), (4) a time agreement and (5) a response (accept, decline, counter offer).

DECLARATION   A declaration is the act of reconstituting a set of relationships. Voicing declarations sculpts identities and defines possibilities (e.g., "I now pronounce you husband and wife"). You shape reality by your declarations.

ASSERTION   An assertion is an interpretation that you can back up with evidence, an affirmation. Asserting is the act of stating a verifiable claim positively.

Those four types of conversation are your tools for intervention. This is not new technology in the sense that every voluntary action that has ever occurred between humans was on the basis of such exchanges. What is new is that we are bringing this dynamic into the foreground so you can see it and begin to use it deliberately. By your speaking—and your listening—you can turn around any situation and further your aspirations by transforming your good ideas into action.

Promises, requests, declarations, and assertions are *performative*— expressions that serve to effect a transaction or that constitute the performance of the specified act by virtue of their utterance. Promise, request, declaration, and assertion are the key categorical words, but there are myriad other words that are also performative. For instance, different types of promises are implied by the words: agree, commit, consent, vow, intend, plan, assure, swear. Even the words refuse and decline are promises—promises *not* to do something. You can make a request with such words as, beg, ask, demand, invite, plead, propose, wish, urge, suggest, require, recommend. As with promises, there are negative requests, such as, forbid and warn. Alternative words for declarations are: resign, nominate, name, confirm, decree, concede, apply, pronounce, acknowledge, love, forgive, trust, recognize, agree. Finally, an assertion can be conveyed by words like maintain, predict, postulate, verify, testify, claim, surmise, submit, deny, argue, conclude, contend. These words are not interchangeable. An invitation is obviously not the same as a demand—they each connote a distinct degree of authority, freedom, and importance. What these words have in common is that their utterance constitutes the performance of the specified act, thereby reconstituting social reality (e.g., "I now pronounce you man and wife," "I swear to repay the loan," "I invite you to join our meeting," "I claim that the educational system is in crisis").

The mere *use* of one of those words does not constitute a meaningful act. The effectiveness of speaking depends on the sincerity and the competence of the speaker. Sincerity—being free from hypocrisy— requires the courage to expose yourself, to make your private conversation public. The courageous act of being sincere means revealing what would otherwise be covered up, thus giving your genuine concerns the chance of being put into action. Competence—the quality or state of having the requisite or adequate ability or qualities—determines the probability for fulfillment of the promise, request, declaration, or assertion. No matter how sincerely you want to do something, your promise is no good unless you are competent to fulfill it. Likewise, making a request of someone who isn't competent to fulfill it is not taking committed action—it doesn't intervene in anything. Lacking sincerity or competence doesn't preclude miracles from happening. On the other hand, we often underestimate our capabilities. But miracles don't exist in the same domain as committed action. You can't count on a miracle to perform the actions that will fulfill your commitments. Promises, requests, declarations, and assertions perform the specified act by virtue of their utterance only when uttered by *sincere* and *competent* speakers.

Promises, requests, declarations, and assertions cause action. In any language, all action occurs through one of these types of conversation.

Not all conversations need to be conversations that intervene and cause action. There are chitchat, fact finding, speculation, assessment, research, brainstorming, and so on. All of those kinds of speaking are appropriate in their place. But, when it is time for intervention, when you need *action*, promises, requests, declarations, and assertions are guaranteed vehicles.

How effective are your speaking and listening?

- Spend the rest of today or all day tomorrow practicing the art of committed speaking. Make all of your requests and promises using the words 'I request' and 'I promise,' and include all of the requirements of complete requests and promises (i.e., 'I request that you do X by Y time,' and 'I promise that I'll Y by Z time'). While it may seem stilted and a bit awkward, I promise that it will make a difference in how effective you are, and in how effective the other people involved are.

- When you listen to people, do you hear when they are making vague or implicit requests and promises? For the next day, practice assisting the people around you to make their requests and promises specific and explicit. For example, if someone at work asks you to handle something, but you aren't sure what the conditions for fulfillment are (i.e., *exactly* what is being asked for and by when), then don't just do what we usually do, which is assume that we know, or pretend that we know, or hope that we can use their vagueness to our advantage as an excuse for not doing what they wanted when they wanted it. Instead, for the next twenty-four hours, don't agree to any requests unless you are crystal clear about what you are promising, and don't accept any promises that aren't specific and complete. You may meet resistance— people hate to give up the back door that being vague represents. Do it anyway. Again, I promise that you and the others involved will be more effective than you ever have been.

- Don't stop the two above techniques after twenty-four hours. If you are clear on complete requests and promises, then begin using the other words that signify requests and promises (i.e., invite, demand, ask, swear, guarantee, and so on). Also begin to identify declarations and assertions and observe their roles in bringing forth reality.

Wake-Up Call

So, you've been reading this book now for a hundred pages or so. Here are some questions to assist you in confronting your commitment:

- What difference have you made in your life out of reading this book?
- Specifically, what is different now about you, your thinking, your behavior, your communication, and your results than before you began this work?
- If I were to ask the people who know you if they notice anything different, what would they say?
- Have you done anything at all in an effort to apply the insights you have had to your life or is this just another gesture?
- What was it that you wanted to accomplish out of this? Have you accomplished it or have you made actual progress toward accomplishing it? If so, acknowledge yourself for the courage and commitment it took to keep your word, and ask yourself 'What's next?' If not, what are you waiting for?

Did you notice how cunning human beings can be? We can fool even ourselves into believing that we are getting something done when all we are doing is performing empty gestures, or "trying."

Human inertia is tenacious. Our reasons for not keeping our word are incredibly creative. Isn't it mind-boggling that we are unwilling or too lazy to do the things that we know will improve the quality of our lives? It is easier to get a camel through the eye of a needle than to get a human being to make a change in his or her behavior. The fact is, being resigned about life is part of being human.

Think seriously about what you are doing here. If you aren't in the trenches shoveling the dirt in order to become who you aspire to be, you might as well go watch reruns of "Fantasy Island" because that's about as close as you'll come to transformation.

A final question: Why bother reading another word?

11

Jim Kelly

GRADUATE PROFILE

"I can say something now that before I never believed when people told me," says Jim Kelly. "The training did, in fact, totally transform my life in five days. People had said that to me, and I said 'Yes, sure, sure.' But I did not really understand how that could be. I have been through many, many experiences that have changed my life; leaving a small town to go to California, going to college, getting married, having children, being appointed to a special post in the government in Washington, DC. But nothing compares. Even all together, those experiences don't come close to comparing with what happened for me from Wednesday evening to Sunday evening in the training."

Jim lives in the Washington, DC, area where he is the president of a business development and representation firm. "We are a consulting firm that provides assistance to companies across the country and overseas that are interested in doing business with the government, or breaking into new business areas with the government." Jim did the Lifespring Basic Training in December of 1987.

"The principal reason I took the training was that I had met a number of people who had taken it and I noticed something very unusual about them. Number one, I was very comfortable with them. Number two, there was interaction among them which was open and honest and free. I found it continuously refreshing. I found myself wanting to go back and be with those people, individually and collectively. In the process of getting to know them better, I found the one common thread was that they had all gone through the Lifespring trainings at various times. As I got closer and closer to them I felt that the relationships I had with them were different than any other relationships I had ever had in my life.

"They were urging me to take advantage of this opportunity and take the Basic Training. For about two or three months, they kept asking me if I was interested and I said yes, but that, between running my business and the activities in my personal life, time was a major obstacle for me. Since I felt my life was going pretty well, I didn't see the urgency in finding the time to do the training.

"When I finally did the training, I was not really sure what I would find, although I did know that there were a number of relationships in my life that I did not feel were at the maximum, particularly involving my children. Also, I was having some lingering difficulties with my business partner. I felt, if I did nothing else but take a look at what there was in those relationships that I might be able to do something about, the training would be important and worthwhile. I entered the Basic Training a little skeptical, but very curious.

"I think maybe I could best illustrate how important the training was for me with an example that is very special to me. One of the relationships in my life that was very, very important to me and will always be important to me is the relationship between my son and me. My father, who is eighty years old, is a very lively, loving, caring, sharing man. For most of my life he has been just about my best friend. I had attempted to have a similar relationship with my son who is now twenty-two years old.

"A couple of years ago, after having spent twenty beautiful years coaching him, teaching him, working with him, traveling with him, being his counselor and friend, he made a decision about his life which I reacted to quite negatively. He decided to drop out of college and concentrate on becoming a musician. A rock musician, at that. I was fortunate enough to have been the only member of my family to ever go to college and I wanted to see all of my children get a college education. My two daughters have done so and my son was well on his way, but dropped out of school after his first year. He came to see me and said that he wanted to change his life. He wanted to work to earn money so that he could study and write music on his own and be a member of a local performing band. He really went into it big. He took a position with Domino's Pizza as a pizza delivery boy. That just about killed me because, while he was in college, he was doing wonderfully as a training assistant in a computer center. He went from that to being a pizza boy because he wanted to have as much free time as possible to write and study and practice his music—music which I didn't find pleasant to listen to. This was more than I could take. So, being the righteous soul that I was, I said I didn't agree and I wouldn't support him despite his pleading with me.

"He moved out and I slowly but surely eased myself out of his life. As time went by, I isolated myself from him more strongly. This happened at the same time my marriage ended. In the process I maintained close contact with my daughters, but eliminated just about any contact with my son. I did it because I felt that was the way in which I could send a message to him so that he would see the light and come back and do things my way.

"As time went on, I got stronger and stronger in my righteousness —and in my isolation. I had become more and more insulated. My daughters were practically the only people who knew my phone number. The year before I did the training, I didn't even celebrate Christmas with my son. Inside it was probably one of the most difficult situations I ever had because of the love I felt for him. But I was completely overtaken by this feeling of how important it was to be right in spite of any other considerations. I was living completely opposite to the way I had believed in and lived for the previous twenty years or so.

"As I went into the Basic Training I focused particularly on the relationship with my son. I wanted to get to the bottom of my own feelings and my approach. I was in search of something that I could do to help *him* see how to change. As I progressed through the Basic, though, I learned many things about myself and how I was living my life that I wasn't willing to look at on my own.

"During the exercise about your mother and father, the importance of my relationship with my father came back to me. I could imagine my son going through the same exercise if he were doing the Basic, and I realized through that experience how important my relationship with my son really was. It was at that point that I really had a major breakthrough because then I began to focus on myself. I began to really look at the way I was showing up in my life and the things I was doing. That, coupled with an exercise in which I saw how overwhelming my need to be right was, how unwilling I was to listen to other points of view, absolutely opened me up to recognize how deeply I love my son and how important it was for me to focus on *my* side of the relationship.

"Then I looked at vulnerability, honesty, and openness. In dealing with those experiences, I made a decision about three-quarters of the way through the training that I was going to totally change my approach to my son the minute I had the opportunity to. Immediately after graduation, I literally ran to a telephone and called him and scheduled an appointment for us to meet the next night. He said to me 'Dad, will you really have time? Will you really show up?' I told him I absolutely would.

"He came to my apartment the next night and stayed with me for a long time. I opened up to him and explained how important it was to me that he be in my life. I discussed with him what I had learned about myself in the training and what I had learned about my love for him and the parallel in my relationship with my father. He told me that he had been waiting for me to tell him that for a long, long time. We put our arms around each other and just held each other for probably the better part of an hour. We talked about the long period of time we had been away from each other and what a waste of time that was. We made a mutual commitment to two things. One was that I would immediately accept and support what he was attempting to do. He in turn agreed to spend much more time with me and to accept what I was going through. That night our relationship reached a new height. Today he is on a tour with a name band and is full of confidence in himself and the future. He sends me notes regularly, always expressing gratitude for the breakthrough in our relationship.

"That experience is really a microcosm of what I did in about ten or fifteen other relationships in my life that I had in one way, shape, or form either sabotaged, abandoned, or let deteriorate. I put a list together of people that I felt I needed to go back to and reopen the relationship. I am still working on that list, but each experience is a whole new awakening and reopening for me.

"Because of the openness and honesty and vulnerability that I'm willing to share, all of which I took from the Basic Training, each and every relationship in my life has been totally enhanced. I have a relationship with a woman in my life which is probably the best of any I have ever had. My working relationship with my business partner has changed. We renegotiated our business arrangement in such a way that it is now on terms that work for us both. At the time I entered the Basic Training, I was considering leaving the partnership. Since then, I have been willing to confront areas of our business relationship which were not working as well as they should in order for the business to be as effective as possible. Equally as important, I have been willing to be much more open and honest with clients. My communication has been better. I have been more candid and forceful when making critical recommendations to them or when discussing with them how strong and committed they need to be in presenting their capabilities to potential customers. My recommendations have been clearer and sharper, my clients' willingness to accept those recommendations has risen, and, in many cases, their effectiveness has improved. I think that all of that has happened because, since the training, my commitment to being successful is stronger; my demand for excellence is higher; my intensity and focus are clearer.

"What else has happened to me is I've become more effective in my use of time. Time, remember, was the issue that I used over and over again for why I would not do the training. I think, in reality, the reason was fear of what I might find, but I didn't figure that out until I was already in the Basic. Before that, time was something that controlled my life. I used to work seven days a week. I now work five or five and a half. I have not worked a Saturday, except on very rare occasions, since I did the Basic. I now find myself needing less sleep, working less, exercising, going outdoors, and doing things I hadn't done for a long time. Getting away from work and integrating recreation and relaxation into my life has relieved a lot of tension and increased my effectiveness in all aspects of life. My relationships are better. My work is more productive. I am more relaxed and more open. I feel healthier, more vital. I am looking for more and more things to do all the time.

"My life is totally different than it was before. I'm open and honest. I now cry in front of people. I now laugh out loud. I am willing to dance in public which I was seldom willing to do before. I am just completely different and am showing up in a completely different way."

Jim talked about the level of risk that he now faces daily. "Washington, DC, is not a town in which you find a lot of risk takers on the street. I have had my share of living in a conformed and confined society. What I am doing is taking risks with people who have not seen me risk before. Being vulnerable and taking risks is not easy. It takes an extra effort all the time to do it, but the value that I find each time makes it easier and easier.

"Having the opportunity in the confines of the training room to experience taking risks was really important to me. Giving someone honest feedback, for instance, risks disapproval. I like to have approval, so that was very big for me in the training. The fear of looking silly, or not being in total control represents risk to me. Being vulnerable was confrontive. Opening myself up to someone, sharing myself in an honest, open way was very risky for me. To let my emotions show was risky and difficult for me. Willingness to just plain stretch and go outside of my comfort zone was difficult for me to do. Just about every aspect of it was risky. It is as a consequence of those experiences that now, in society, I'm more and more willing to risk. The returns for the risks I'm taking are really infinite.

"I believe I've become a more interesting person to know. I get more involved with every aspect of a conversation. I'm not always talking about one thing—work. I'm listening more. My effectiveness as a listener has just become tremendous. I find myself now sitting and listening and being fascinated at what I hear from other people from all walks of life. I've learned more from listening in the last four months than I ever had before.

"I really value the numerous people that have come into my life by way of the training, including the staff at Lifespring. Their sensitivity and enthusiasm and commitment are a continuous inspiration to me. I can't begin to say how important I think that is here in Washington, DC. This is a very, very powerful city. It is also a city that is asleep in many ways. The potential for what can be accomplished in this city is significantly enhanced by the existence of Lifespring trainings.

"The other evening, I was talking with an individual who was considering enrolling in the Basic Training. He was concerned about the cost. He is a man about my age, who also has some children. I told him the story of how the training transformed my relationship with my son. I said that on that basis alone, I would say that the value of that training would be at least several hundred thousand dollars or several million dollars, I wasn't sure which. Either way, it is one of the best bargains anyone could ever have."

12

I Give You My Word

YOUR WORD

There is a familiar saying: "Talk is cheap." Consider the possibility that talk is powerful, but we have cheapened it by not living by our word. Speech has tremendous power to evoke, inspire, and create—it is in itself effective action.

Take a look at how you hold giving your word.

- On a scale of 0–10, how important is keeping your word?
- Is your word your bond?

Most people would say, yes, they are good for their word and keeping it rates an 11 in importance. But look past that easy answer to what your actions actually reflect. How often do you tell someone you will call them, and don't? How often do you say you will do something, when you mean you'll try? How often do you make a promise in order to get the approval or acceptance of others? How often do you make an agreement out of impatience, just to "get on with things"? How often do you hope that your children do as you say, not as you do?

What percentage of the promises that you make to other people do you keep? What percentage of the promises you make to yourself do you keep? The average is that people keep anywhere from 30 to 99 percent of their promises to other people and from 10 to 60 percent of their promises to themselves. Let's take an example with an above average response. Say you keep 75 percent of the agreements you make overall. That means that 25 percent of the time you cannot be counted on by yourself or others. When you break a promise you probably have a good reason, but the fact remains that your overall reliability is only 75 percent.

Not keeping all of your promises does not imply that you are insincere, incompetent, or untrustworthy. It simply means that you don't keep all of your promises. Even the most conscientious of us falters when it comes to making and keeping agreements. People have breakdowns. However, no matter how consistent or inconsistent you are about keeping your promises, reevaluating and transforming how you hold giving your word will make a difference in your effectiveness and in the quality of your life.

What is the significance of "your word"? When we speak of language, we mean more than a system of symbols and representations; our language contains our whole structure of interpretation (the framework or machinery that governs what we think and feel) and communication (how we express what we think and feel). All human action occurs within the domain of language. In essence, through our speaking and listening we bring forth reality. For example, when you make a promise, your life begins to flow in a new direction out of what you've spoken. Perhaps you tell a friend that you will give him a ride to the airport on Saturday morning. Then all of your subsequent actions take that promise into account, directly influencing the future for yourself and others. Giving your word, by setting new conversation and new action in motion, is a fundamental element of the progress of human history.

DECLARATIONS

Not all conversations *directly* produce action. But any declaration has the potential to generate reality. If, for instance, you express your opinion to an associate that he can't be trusted, you have not merely expressed an opinion, you have issued a verdict. You have given him that identity, and may close down many possibilities by continuing to deal with him from that characterization. Then, if you voice that opinion to someone else, possibilities may close down for yourself, your associate, and anyone else you tell. Thus, sometimes your assessments can take on the status of facts. The same is often true of declarations made about you. Let's say when you were young a teacher said you were a slower student than the other kids. But, let's say that you just had bad eyesight and couldn't see the blackboard; this caused you, in fact, to exhibit the behavior of a slow student. Although your vision problem may be discovered and corrected, the attitudes and practices that you took on as a result of being declared a slow learner may pose a problem that is much more intractable than your vision problem. Similarly, declarations you make for yourself shape reality. "I am a teacher," "I am worried," "I am sick," "I am good/bad at that," are nothing more than assessments that become facts by virtue of your declaration.

What is true about declarations is that you can make new ones, thereby reclaiming possibilities for yourself and others. In some cases, it can be as simple as redeclaring (e.g., you can renew your relationship with the associate you believed was untrustworthy by retracting your opinion or voicing a new possibility to him and anyone else you spoke to). Of course, it takes more than the utterance of words to shed a characterization that has been abided by and reinforced over the years (e.g., our "slow learner"), but once a commitment is declared, you can research and adopt the behaviors that move you forward in a new direction. Speaking a declaration begins the process of redirecting your actions. Through your declarations, your spoken word is a tool for closing out inappropriate self-characterizations and reclaiming the possibilities available to you. If you honor your word as a causal agent, you heighten your effectiveness and your power to re-invent yourself through your speaking.

Explore the following questions and decide for yourself the power of language. Write your thoughts in your journal.

- In the public domain, think of what it would be like if politicians, world leaders, educators, business kingpins, and other influential figures lived by the following rule: 'When I say it, it happens, and if I don't say it, it doesn't happen.' Imagine a magic wand which only allows what is specifically spoken to become reality and automatically manifests exactly what is spoken. Do you think the communication of public figures would transform both in terms of content and effectiveness?
- In the private domain, how would your communication be if you followed the same rule? If everything you spoke became reality exactly as you spoke it? If only that which you specifically declared happened?
- How much of what you hear on the news, in the office, in your home, do you really listen to seriously?

Try this experiment for a day. Listen to yourself and others with an "innocent" ear, as though you and they actually mean *exactly* what you say, no more, no less. Listen for how authentic people's speaking is. Listen especially to the authenticity of your own speaking. How much of your communication is a recital of a semi-automatic, insincere script? How rigorously have you thought out what you say; for instance, could you give valid evidence to substantiate your points-of-view if you were questioned? How much of your communication actually produces any effective action, causing tangible, measurable results? While you're at it, also try to remain silent at times when you are only making noise, filling space with meaningless words, spouting off opinions you can't substantiate with evidence, or gossiping. Notice how much of our speaking is wasted. You will quickly see how we have gotten to the point where talk has been made cheap. You will also be able to see that talk isn't inherently cheap, but rather, we have robbed it of its inherent power.

PSYCHOLOGICAL ASSESSMENT VS. INTERVENTION

Beware of the ever so enticing "psychological assessment." A psychological assessment is a judgment or a statement that merely reflects the speaker's opinions. They are interpretations that are not based on facts. The speaker's motivation for stating them is to be right and to look good; they either accomplish nothing or they actually hinder effective action and success. Akin to gossip, psychological assessment imposes the speaker's agenda on other people or situations. While all of our interpretations embody our underlying prejudices and biases, psychological assessments glorify our subjective opinions and express them as though they were facts.

The distinction between a valid assertion intended to further a situation by intervening in it and a psychological assessment is a subtle one. The statement "Jane is a liar" may be based on facts and may be intended to caution someone who is considering working on a project with Jane. Or, it may be a rumor, gossip, or an assessment made by the speaker that is not intended to contribute anything worthwhile. One way to identify a psychological assessment is to ask the speaker (yourself in many cases) what evidence he or she has to back up the claim. If the individual (or you) has no evidence, says he/she heard it from someone else, just has a feeling, can tell, or can "read" people intuitively, it is a psychological assessment. Other relevant questions are "What was the speaker's purpose in making that comment?" or "What did the speaker want to accomplish?" Usually, in the case of psychological assessments, the speaker's motivation is to be right and to look good at someone or something else's expense.

There is no way not to have psychological assessments; like our bodies, they are part of the human condition. But confusing them with productive communication impedes effective action. Voicing psychological assessments distracts people's attention from the project at hand, sidetracking energy into a conversation that will not render action. Further, when you speak psychological assessments, you muck up the clarity of purpose necessary to be effective by interjecting irrelevant, baseless, and often damaging, claims. Finally, if you focus on psychological assessments, you block your vision of the available possibilities by crowding your space with useless trivia—your ability to see possibilities is obscured like your vision is obscured when mud splashes on your windshield. We have psychological assessments, but we are not trained to discern them from valuable assertions. Hence, we waste a lot of time, thought, and conversation on vain, useless hot air while thinking that we are doing something worthwhile. When we analyze people's conversations according to their motivation and what they get accomplished, we find that often they think, or hope, that they are intervening, making something productive happen or are somehow making a valuable contribution, when they are really just spouting their opinions, judgments, and positions.

ACTION THROUGH WORDS

Psychological assessments can disguise themselves in many different kinds of communications and the same statement can in one context be a psychological assessment while in another context it is a constructive communication. We make a lot of noise about our psychological assessments, giving us the impression that something is happening when actually the opposite is true—some possibility is actually being prevented. As we have previously discussed at length, there are types of conversation that generate action rather than throttle it, words that perform action merely by their utterance.

Simply put, the nature of a conversation that produces action is that you place your own buns right on the firing line. In other words, you commit yourself by making specific promises, requests, declarations and assertions, leaving yourself no back doors, and you accept no less from others. You end up with a clear sense of where you are going in a project and a way to recognize when you are in breakdown and when you are complete. Often, just the process of clarifying requests and promises involves creativity and concentration that directly furthers the project at hand.

Of course, explicit requests are more likely to be declined than vague ones. But, would you rather have someone agree to a vague request, and then not produce the goods as you "expected," or would you rather know up front that someone is unwilling or unable to carry out your request? Similarly, are you more comfortable making a precise promise, or agreeing to an ambiguous request and hoping that you will satisfy the expectations? Declining someone's request, or being declined certainly is not one of life's greatest pleasures, but it can actually further you in accomplishing the results that matter to you. A clear and responsible decline saves you from the deadly illusion that you are getting something done when, in fact, you are not. It forces you to find the right person for the right job. Likewise, insisting that requests made of you be specific allows you to take on only the projects that are aligned with your principles and your abilities.

PROMISES AND REQUESTS: SPEAKING THAT INTERVENES AND PRODUCES ACTION

Before you can get on the field and play baseball, you have to learn the rules of the game. Similarly, before you can have a conversation that intervenes and produces action, you must be clear on the elements of such a conversation. In their simplest form, conversations for intervention consist primarily of promises and requests. To review, a complete request or promise includes: (1) a speaker, (2) a listener, (3) specific terms for fulfillment (exactly what will be produced), (4) time agreement (by when it will be produced), and (5) a response (accept, decline, offer an alternative). There are different gradients of requests (invitation, demand, suggestion, proposal, etc.). In all cases, the person of whom the request is being made must have the option to decline with dignity. Otherwise, it is not a request and won't necessarily generate effective action. Likewise, with promises there are many levels (promise, vow, agree, etc.). If someone breaks a promise he or she made to you, questioning the person's integrity will not solve your problem. If someone makes an insincere promise, then the source of the breakdown lies back in the conversation in which you made the request and/or accepted that person's promise in the first place, not with the individual's subsequent actions. If you face such a breakdown, identify what didn't work, evaluate the person's competence to fulfill your request or promise, and make a new agreement. When you have conversations of requests and promises, those interactions reconstitute your relationships with people. The more specific you are with your requests and your promises, the more you support the integrity of all involved and the higher the chances for accomplishment.

Being specific does not mean that fulfilling the agreement will be easier or more fun. The work to be done is still the work to be done. In fact, tension usually rises as you nail down specific expectations. In the long run, however, the certainty of expectations and the sense of completion when agreements are fulfilled far surpasses the temporary relief of escaping full and precise commitment.

When the terms of the project are clear, breakdowns are more obvious, thus opening up the possibilities for resolution. Conversely, if the parameters of a project are unclear, flaws and mistakes are either not noticed or are easily covered up, thereby preventing resolution and sabotaging the project.

Requests and promises produce action because they elicit or manifest commitment. They set action in motion, action that will intervene in the future causing something to happen that may not otherwise have happened.

This isn't new—people make requests and promises all the time, and have forever. However, in unexamined interactions, we are generally unaware of the powerful dynamics of promises and requests. Bringing to the foreground the implicit power of certain types of speaking, namely promises and requests, gives you necessary technology to advance your projects, resolve breakdowns, and generate action through your communication.

THE VULNERABILITY OF COMMITTING YOURSELF

Implicit in commitment is vulnerability. There is no way to be committed without being at risk by virtue of your commitment. Putting yourself on the line, pinning yourself down with exactitude, being passionate about something, leaves you vulnerable. You are putting your very identity at stake by openly declaring yourself through your commitments. Commitment requires courage. You must be willing to face being unsuccessful or just plain wrong. In committing yourself you forfeit your opportunity to blend in with the mob, to tag onto the coattails of a winner, or to switch loyalties without anyone else noticing. Being committed opens you up to being challenged, accused, and ridiculed.

Commitment requires rigorous self-examination. Although it may be impossible to be absolutely clear about your values, continually exploring what is important to you assists you to express your commitment in words and actions that are accurate and that strengthen your sense of integrity. When you are challenged, you can support your case with solid confidence and clear, thoughtful arguments rather than giving a blustery defense of an opinion you have not really thought through yourself. You can modify your point of view efficiently and meaningfully rather than changing your mind at the drop of a feather with no better reasons than those upon which your previous point of view was based. Commitment demands that you think about what you do and why you do it.

What does it take to be committed in a way that works?

First, you have to "be a stand for commitment." Commitment for its own sake must be worthwhile to you. Floundering around waiting for the ultimate in perfect commitments is not being committed. But neither is tying yourself to causes that aren't meaningful to you; you must choose commitments that embody your major concerns and that you can embrace wholeheartedly. Being a stand for commitment is a general way of being, but it is also something that you can practice by making specific commitments. At some point, you must simply commit yourself, and then be committed to your commitments, make decisions according to what will best further those particular commitments.

Second, scrutinize your values and concerns; discover what really matters to you. Your commitments have a chance of lasting and being a source of deep fulfillment only if they align with your priorities in life.

Third, be willing to declare unequivocally what you stand for, and to risk the vulnerability that comes with taking such a stand. Go public about your commitments.

Fourth, be rigorous and specific about your words and actions. Loosely and loudly throwing around words like "commitment" and "declaration" does not a commitment make. You've got to back up your ideas with action. Look to your words and actions and you will see what you are *really* committed to.

Finally, be frank about what actually happens. Your actual results provide the best tangible data for evaluating your effectiveness and for correcting yourself.

Answer the questions below in your journal to clarify your commitments.

- What is important to you regarding your family, work, health, wealth, relationships, and so on?
- What are your commitments regarding your family, work, health, wealth, relationships, and so on (i.e., the end state or goal for the future that is governing your current behavior)?
- Is your behavior effectively leading toward the fulfillment of those commitments? In what ways is it or isn't it?
- Do your results demonstrate that your actions in each domain are, in fact, effective? If not, what results specifically demonstrate that you are not being effective? In those particular areas, what is missing and what is next for you (i.e., what action will you take now to move forward?)?

KEEPING YOUR WORD / BREAKING YOUR WORD

When and why do you give your word? In Lifespring courses we have a process during which all participants are requested to agree to a series of ground rules. If they will not give their word to play by these rules, they may not take the training. We typically lose a few who are unwilling to participate according to the rules of the training. Of those who choose to continue the training, having agreed to the rules, over 80 percent admit to having broken at least one of the rules after only two days of the training. Why? Some "forgot" the rules, some didn't pay attention to what they were agreeing to the first night, some were rebelling against authority, some were seeking confrontation and attention. Why did these people give their word in the first place? Some genuinely intended to play by the rules, some just wanted to get on with things in their own way, others wanted to avoid the hassle of questioning the rules or declining to agree to them. The reasons go on and on. These people were willing to give their word to themselves and the rest of the group, and to accept everyone else's word to play by the same rules. What happened? We want everyone else to keep their word with us, but we think we are the exception to the rule. What matters aren't the reasons people break their word, it is how people value giving their word in the first place.

What possibilities do you close when you break your word? You lose self-esteem, self-confidence, self-respect, and credibility in the eyes of others. You question your own integrity, cause confusion, and others get the message that you cannot be counted on. Regardless of how good your excuse is for breaking an agreement with someone, people get the message that they don't matter to you. You get stuck in incompletion, self-doubt, unkept promises, and their corresponding emotional states. The possibilities available in your relationships with yourself and others steadily narrow.

When you break your word, you can always say you're sorry, right? It takes a big person to say he or she is sorry, or so we say. Apologizing repairs any damage you have caused, doesn't it? Or does it? Do you notice that some people apologize for the same things over and over again, or that when you apologize to people it is often repeatedly over the same issue? Given the choice between "I'm sorry" and something else, wouldn't you prefer something like, "You can count on me not to let this happen again"; or "Next time, you can count on me to handle that in this way . . . "; or "I acknowledge that I broke a promise. From this moment on you can count on me to . . . "? Apologies are appropriate, but they don't necessarily imply a commitment to correction or to different behavior in the future.

What possibilities open up when you keep your word? The reverse of all of the prices you pay for breaking your word comes out of keeping your word. Your potential for being in relationships that are based on integrity increases. People may not always like you, but out of knowing they can count on you to keep your word they will tend to respect you and honor your word. It is empowering for people to be around your high degree of integrity, whether they like you or not. When you keep your word to yourself and others, your self-esteem, self-confidence, and self-respect go up. You reinforce your personal effectiveness and your ability to turn your intentions into action.

Possibilities are opened and closed on the other side of the picture as well. For instance, there are rewards for *not* keeping your word. People stop asking you to make promises. You are free of obligations. You get attention. You have an excuse to slack off and avoid greater responsibility.

Some of the consequences of keeping your word can be interpreted as prices you pay. Your expectations of yourself increase as you consistently fulfill your promises. Others expect more of you and are less likely to accept excuses from you. Since you are motivated to live as your word and not to have people approve of you, some people may not like you.

Since we are not robots, and there isn't a person alive who always keeps his or her word, address this issue by acknowledging what works and what doesn't work rather than judging right and wrong. What is your relationship with your word? Write your responses in your journal.

- What possibilities open up for you when you make a promise?
- What possibilities close when you make a promise?
- What behavior do you exhibit when you break your word? When someone breaks their word with you? What behavior would serve better?
- What behavior do you exhibit when you keep your word? When others keep their word with you? What behavior would serve better?
- What prices and rewards might you face if you became more rigorous about your word?

COMMITMENTS, WORDS, ACTIONS

Effective conversations for intervention bring commitments to light. What is commitment? Let's start by naming what is *not* commitment. I say commitment is not an idea about how you would like something to be; it is not a wish, hope, or dream; it's not hype; it's not loyalty or obedience; it isn't self-sacrifice; it's not compulsion or drive; it isn't positive thinking; and it isn't intention.

Commitment is an end state or goal in the future that governs your behavior in the present. The nature of your commitment shows up in your words and actions. But saying that commitment shows up in your words and actions doesn't mean that every activity is a meaningful commitment. Commitment isn't a thing or an activity, but a part of your identity. For instance, saying "I do" doesn't make you a wife or husband except in a purely superficial, academic sense. That you *are* the commitment to *being* a husband or a wife shows up in your *words* and *actions* from the moment you say "I do." Discipline yourself to think of your commitment as what is demonstrated in your actions. Begin to look to the feedback of the physical universe, your actual results, to tell you what commitment you are. As you begin to see that you *are* your commitments, as manifested in your words and actions, adjust your words and actions so that you are operating with integrity.

Skip Williams

GRADUATE PROFILE

When Skip Williams first heard about the Basic Training, he was interested, but skeptical. "I was at a point in my life where, although good things were happening in my life, particularly in my work, I was looking for something else—something to connect me spiritually with myself and with other people. When a co-worker told me about the trainings, I was immediately interested. However, one of the things that really bothered me as we began to talk about it a little bit more was I thought this was either one of these white, middle-class gimmicks, or something for people who needed to be fixed." Skip, an anesthesiologist, intensive care unit co-director, and professor at George Washington University Hospital, is black. He was born in Harlem and raised in Brooklyn. The woman who told him about the trainings offered to introduce him to a black man who was a graduate of the training. "They came by my house one Sunday afternoon. It turns out that this man not only was black, but was also from Brooklyn. He said he felt the trainings were probably the most significant thing that had happened to him in his life. He related personal experiences about how it had affected his relationship with his wife and family and how he had a richer, fuller life as a result. I felt that this guy was being really honest with me, and I knew I could trust my friend who first told me about Lifespring, so I said 'Why not?'

"I went into the training with nervous anticipation. I had no idea what was going to happen. I had never gone to a Guest Event. I was reluctant and nervous. During the first evening, I sat there wondering why I was doing this.

"By the second night, I was beginning to think there was something to the training, but the most significant thing that occured for me was what they call the Red/Black Game on the third night. Looking at how I participated in that game was a big slap in the face. I came face to face with some issues that I thought I had taken care of in my life, but had obviously not. That exercise opened up incredible possibilities for me, particularly with respect to my father. I played the game knowing how to win. I made my statement to the group and I fought for about ten minutes. Then my attitude was 'Forget it!' Nobody was listening. Everybody wanted to fight. Forget it. I sat there and kept my mouth shut. I extrapolated that and realized that I did the same thing in other areas of my life too.

"The context of the Basic Training gave me the perfect opportunity to deal with issues of vulnerability in that I could say the things that I was really feeling in my heart. In the past, I wouldn't always say those things in case people criticized me for them or wouldn't like me as a result. I always either gave in to make people feel good, or hid that vulnerability and acted like I didn't care at all. That was one major breakthrough that resulted from the Red/Black Game. I decided that from that point on, if a thousand people were saying one thing and I felt strongly about a different thing, as long as I wasn't being dogmatic I would stick to what I believed was right. That has spilled over into my everyday life now.

"Another result of the Red/Black experience was that I contacted my father, from whom I had been estranged for over twenty years. What allowed me to do that was that in the training I felt I was with the most caring, supportive people. That environment was so nurturing, so caring, that it really gave me strength. I got a chance to really relate with what it was like for my father. I looked back and acknowledged that he really didn't know how to be a father. And lots of fathers don't know how to be fathers. And I'm not sure if I would know how to be a father, either. That was a real release for me. It really helped me be comfortable with my relationship with my dad. As I was dialing his number, I was shaking. I told him that I knew we had had a lousy relationship and, although I still disagree with a lot of the things that he's done, he's my father and I love him. I was able to say that for the first time in twenty years. Since that time we talk to each other at least on a weekly basis. We've seen each other several times and we're beginning to work out a relationship again.

"Another thing I looked at in the training was leadership. I had always been characterized as a leader, but I was a reluctant leader. As a result of the trainings, I actually realized what it means to be a leader. What it means to really take responsibility. Although I can't please everybody, at the same time I can be who I am and continue to make the important decisions that I need to make for other people as well as myself.

"That has really been valuable to me in terms of giving lectures. One of the things I have wanted was to be recognized as an excellent teacher. People have always said I was a good teacher and a good doctor. But one of my goals coming out of the training was to make myself the best teacher that I could possibly be. A week ago I won what we call here the Golden Apple Award. I was voted the most outstanding professor by the students. This is the first time someone in our department has won that award. That is a concrete result that I definitely attribute to the Lifespring trainings. I had wanted it years before and it didn't happen. After the training, I felt that I had more of an inner confidence that came out of the whole aspect of spirituality, of not being an isolated entity. I experienced really feeling connected, that I really had something that was worthwhile to give to people. And, in fact, people commented on how I was different, how my lectures were different. They noticed a surge of confidence that they hadn't seen before. That was very important to me. I was always good in one-on-one situations, but the large group situation always intimidated me a bit. Now, even though I'm intimidated a little, I go ahead and I do whatever is necessary.

"My friendships have been enhanced like they never have been before, both with the true friends I have gained as a result of the trainings, and with my friends who have not done the training. It was a little difficult at first with the friends who hadn't done the trainings because I began to say things that a lot of them really didn't want to hear. One of the goals I set for myself was to be honest in every situation. That goal came out of an exercise in the Basic where I wasn't completely honest with someone. She knew I wasn't being honest, and I could just see the pain in her eyes. Sometimes my commitment to honesty means that I say something to somebody that they may not want to hear. It takes courage, but if it's an honest appraisal, I have to say it. I have a genuine caring and love for the friends I have made through the trainings. These are the kind of friends that I can count on to require the best of me, even if that means confronting me.

"The trainings allowed me to come face to face with who I am and what I really believe in. Even if you never take the trainings, there are certain things you really believe in. The trainings allowed me to take a stand about what I believe in and live my life according to that stand. They have helped me to integrate that in my everyday life by giving me a focal point, a clarity about what I stand for. Through the trainings, I see myself in a position to make a difference."

Risk, Freedom and Success

14

RISK AND FREEDOM

As a free individual, when you take your own initiative, you inevitably risk failure. Just as there is the possibility for success in life, there is a great deal of room for failure. Individual liberty is a marvelous idea, and a good idea is a worthy place to begin. But *being* a possibility, identifying yourself as a possibility, *living* as a possibility— this is the direct result of the risks you take in life. Built into the very possibility of freedom is risk—the possibility of loss or injury.

There are positive and negative kinds of risks. How do you distinguish the sort of risk that opens up possibilities from a mere gamble? We aren't interested in risk for risk's sake. The risk that will serve you is the risk that enables you to further what you are really up to in your life—the risk that forces you to recognize the disparity between your deepest concerns and what your actions are producing, and to close that gap. The only potential for breakthrough —the only thing that will always catapult you from your present situation, from your blindness, from your transparency—is your own experience of seeing what you are really about, the risk of telling yourself the truth.

Consider the following questions. Write your responses in your journal.

- What is your interpretation of individual liberty?
- What is your interpretation of freedom?
- What are the prices and rewards of freedom?
- What is your interpretation of risk?
- What are the prices and rewards of risking?
- Where do you see that your freedom is limited in a way that is out of your control? Could that be merely a matter of interpretation?
- What risks do you find easy to take? Which ones do you avoid at all costs?
- What risks have you been unwilling to take to accomplish what is important to you?
- What are your concerns about risking? What is the down side of risk?
- When have you risked and 'succeeded'? Be specific about your relationships, business, and so on.
- When have you risked and 'failed'? Again, be specific.
- At what general degree of being 'at risk' do you operate every day?

SUCCESS

Because of the competitive nature of our society, Americans often confuse having the objective symbols of success with living a committed, satisfying life. Another point of view on success and failure is that once you get clear about your fundamental concerns, and once you fully commit yourself to those concerns in your actions, then you realize what really counts. What is most effective and harmonious is living out of that commitment. If you are successful in doing this, then you will likely be as successful as possible in the objective sense. If you know who you are and what you're up to in your life, you can play the material game, but your source of fulfillment and empowerment isn't a material scorecard.

The trouble with talking about success is that success is a judgment, an evaluation about what has already happened, a comparison of yourself and others based primarily on material standards. Unfortunately, merely accumulating the symbols of success doesn't guarantee you an experience of personal success.

Thinking of success in terms of your *performance* provides constant motivation. Thinking of success in terms of the accumulation of wealth and power is an endless, futile grind. Operating on the leading edge, participating in your projects passionately and effectively, and living life out of the stand you have taken about what is possible for humankind—that is inspiring. A winning score on the scoreboard after the final gun doesn't necessarily constitute an experience of success, and can be a hollow, short-lived victory. As Gerry Beemiller, a Lifespring graduate who is a self-made millionaire, explains, he made a major career move years ago when he noticed a competitor driving in a Mercedes while he was in a Ford LTD. Now he has his Mercedes. "It doesn't matter to me anymore. I don't really care. It's a nice car to have because I spend so much time behind the wheel, but it isn't the fact that it's a Mercedes that turns me on anymore. Once you've got it, it isn't as important."

There is something missing in the conversation our culture has about success. That conversation, which urges us to develop an image of success through its symbols ("He who dies with the most toys wins") does not address our fundamental cares and concerns as human beings. Does that mean that material success and achieving results are illegitimate or trivial goals? Not at all. Rather, looking to those symbols to give your life meaning doesn't work. Homes, cars, stock portfolios, resumés, being invited to the right parties, and so on, are gratifying in one domain of satisfaction. On a more meaningful level, however, the path toward achieving those symbols more powerfully affects the quality of your life than the symbols themselves. An "ends justify the means" approach to success, even when legal and moral, neglects the significance of the *journey* which is the actual process of *living*.

There is an opening in a conversation about peak performance, a conversation that encourages you to operate as if 100 percent is possible 100 percent of the time. Being committed to maximum participation rather than to a bank balance or a winning record is empowering and vital. And don't you notice that often those people who strive for peak peformance are also the people attaining the material trappings of success? It's not a lucky coincidence. While the proverbial rat race is a grind and no accomplishment is ever enough, living every moment as though your life depended on it is invigorating and rewarding.

When your ambition is motivated by commitment to your ideals you are operating from a stronger, more powerful place than if you're motivated by the desire to acquire the symbols of success. There are countless testimonials in recent bestsellers focusing on business and management success to substantiate this. Those men and women who make it to the top most often get there as a by-product of a dedication to something bigger than their acquisitive nature, like achieving personal excellence or contributing to mankind. By reframing your concept of success and failure, you will be as effective as possible by acting out of lucid and total commitment to your expressed ideals.

Fulfillment has everything to do with your interaction with others. I don't experience myself as successful when I have negotiated a great contract, or bought a new home, or won a tennis match. I experience success when I know I have participated in something with all of my passion, vulnerability, and commitment. Gandhi said: "Full effort is full victory." My accomplishments always, without exception, involve other people. Every accomplishment I have ever achieved, in or out of the work environment, somehow has included other people. Success hinges around how you are with people. Success always includes opening doors for others, standing not only for achieving an intended result, but also for contributing to someone else's experience of personal success.

When you as an individual take a stand about success that integrates the principles of freedom, risking, and acting on your highest ideals, you serve society as a whole. In justifying a society that protects individual liberty, philosophers claim that, insofar as you maxamize liberty, you maximize the possibility for creativity, innovation, personal enterprise, and so on. In the end, the whole society benefits. But a libertarian society will only flourish to the extent that its members are willing to take the risks required for a fruitful exercise of their freedoms. For instance, those individuals who struggled for civil rights throughout American history—before, during, and after the 1960s—risked the possibility of loss and injury for the sake of greater personal and social gains. Their success (although far from complete even now) opened new possibilities for freedom in being human.

Look at success for yourself by answering the questions below in your journal.

- What does success mean to you?
- When you are ninety years old, looking back on your life, what do you think will be more important to you, the symbols you acquired and the image you maintained, or the experience of having given life everything you had?
- How do other people fit into your picture of success? Do you tend to see people as means to an end, or appreciate them regardless of their utility to you?

VULNERABILITY

A key to allowing individual liberty and initiative to flourish is a tolerance, acceptance, and concern for others that is often missing in a competitive culture. Such a climate allows people to take the risk of being vulnerable and open, to share with each other both their faults and highest ideals. One of the most difficult risks that we have to confront is being vulnerable with one another. We find it difficult to take a stand for what we are really concerned with, or to be true to our personal ideals, because we are aware of what others will think.

Taking the risk of being vulnerable creates or deepens a connection between people. Relationships develop a private dimension when people are vulnerable with each other. Through risking being vulnerable, you reconstitute your relationships with people, and thereby your social reality. Take the example of romance. When two people are dating, something almost palpable happens to the relationship when they first kiss. A new sphere of relatedness is born in the public space between them, a "for us" or "between us" that doesn't exist one moment, but does exist in the next moment. When you are vulnerable, you extend a hand of trust, creating a private "for us" that isn't characteristic of most interactions.

Of course, risking and vulnerability don't only bear on love relationships. Suppose you and I are in a meeting together. I am a spy. You know I'm a spy and I know that you know it. And you know that I know that you know I'm a spy. When we meet there is never any mention of my being a spy even though it is common knowledge. At the end of this particular meeting, however, when I stand up to leave, my shirt gets caught on the edge of the table, ripping it so that the wiring hidden inside is exposed. In that instant, our whole relationship is transformed from "I know you know" to "We know."

The Lifespring trainings provide a context in which people can count on the attention, support, and sincere concern of others leaving you fortified to go out in the world, where that attention and concern isn't always present. Being vulnerable is being open to attack or damage. The training provides a solid and unshakable experience of affirmation that you can take with you wherever you go. You experience the possibilities that open up when you risk being authentic in the face of your fear. Your challenge is to create this context in your own interaction with people, both by risking vulnerability yourself and by truly allowing others the freedom to be vulnerable with you.

Reflect on the following questions and record your thoughts in your journal.

- What does vulnerability mean to you?
- What is at stake when you are vulnerable with someone?
- Are the potential rewards of risk and vulnerability worth the potential prices?
- In what area of your life is your unwillingness to be vulnerable holding you back. What actions will you take to break through that barrier?

RISKING IN YOUR OWN LIFE

The United States' Declaration of Independence states that you have a natural and inalienable right to the pursuit of happiness. I believe that you also have a natural and inalienable right to the pursuit of possibilities. Recognizing and acting on your possibilities requires a courageous commitment to your principles, a willingness to risk total failure, acceptance of every other individual's equal right to freedom, and a degree of vulnerability that could end up making you look like a complete fool.

The following are requests about risking in your life. If you accept the requests, consider two suggestions: (1) Use the opportunity to have breakthroughs in your life. One way to know whether you have chosen significant risks is by how reluctant you are to carry them out. Obviously, don't choose risks that are life threatening, but don't let yourself off without pushing your personal limits either. (2) Pick someone to support you in carrying them out. Tell that person what you are promising to do, and ask him or her to follow up with you—to call you every day and ask if you have completed your promises. If, for example, your risk involves meeting new people, promise your supporter that every day you will have conversations with at least two new people whom you find attractive, and that part of those conversations will include an invitation to do something with you. Then, set up a time every day when you will check in with your supporter. Don't make him or her pay for their commitment to you—if you break your word, don't penalize them for it by resisting their support.

The following requests are to promote risks that make a positive difference in your life. Record your promises in your journal.

- Take a risk in your primary relationship. Do you accept or decline? If you accept, what is the risk and when will you have taken it?
- Take a risk at work. Accept or decline? If you accept, what is the risk and when will you have taken it?
- Take a risk with at least one member of your family (the family you grew up with). Accept or decline? If you accept, what is the risk and when will you have taken it?
- Take a risk with at least one friend. Accept or decline? If you accept, what is the risk and when will you have taken it?

This will be a huge challenge for most people because it requires you to do things publicly that are atypical of your usual behavior patterns, and are, therefore, likely to be uncomfortable. I encourage you to jump into the challenge. What you do won't feel natural, and while you are in the process, you may find yourself in self-judgment. One opportunity for breakthrough is when you are on the edge between going back to your same, old way of being and a new possibility. You will be awkward and self-conscious, but choose the path of the new possibility.

15

Gerry Beemiller

GRADUATE PROFILE

Gerry Beemiller is a self-made, successful business executive. He is stimulated by his work, happily married, has beautiful children, lives on a hundred-acre ranch in a house that he designed, drives a Mercedes, and is a respected leader in his community. Gerry, CEO of a Silicon Valley company that represents electronics manufacturers in the marketplace, has all the symbols of success. He also has the *experience* of success—*he knows* that he makes a difference. Because of the stand Gerry has taken about his purpose in life, he seeks opportunities to be successful by contributing to others rather than merely accumulating wealth.

Participating in the Lifespring trainings in 1979 began to shift Gerry's stance about himself. Gerry remembers, "I still look back on the course as having a profound effect on my life. I experienced some ideas of myself that I've never had an opportunity to experience before and saw possibilities for myself that I had never seen. I don't know any other way to do it. Although it can be really challenging at times, it can certainly be rewarding as well."

Gerry's recent project was the second annual Silicon Valley Charity Ball which he created.

The Charity Ball first occurred to Gerry when he and his wife threw a party for their friends, mostly other electronics industry executives. One of those friends pointed to all of the Mercedes, Jaguars, and Rolls Royces pulling in and asked why he hadn't seen all those people at local fund-raising events. This got Gerry thinking, and soon led to his creating the Silicon Valley Charity Ball. "I had to admit that we were not contributing at those events and we weren't seeking opportunities to give. I started thinking about how I could improve the image of the Silicon Valley business community, which, except for a few like the Hewlett and Packard families, isn't known for its philanthropic efforts. I wanted to provide an opportunity for the people who work and live in the valley to give something back to the community in which we have prospered.

"The first year we raised $90,000 for local charities. This year, we raised $220,000. Now my vision is to raise $1 million in one night in Santa Clara County, which has never been done before. I think that within two or three years we'll do that. Now I'm trying to get people to buy into this vision of raising $1 million in one night.

"In the training I got to see that I live in a 'can do' world and most everyone else lives in an 'I can't' world. Before the training, friends would tell me that their relationship with me was a difficult relationship. I was not very sympathetic to friends who would try to sell me their excuses about why they couldn't do things—I wouldn't buy their limiting stories. After the training, I am still clear that you either have the results or you have the reasons why not, but I also see that making people wrong doesn't work. Telling the truth is vital, and now that I am more conscious about *how* I tell it, I am more effective at supporting my friends.

"I'm also a lot better at clearing myself when I get confused or off purpose. We all get stuck. My ability to rebound quickly and get back on track again has saved me a lot of stress and wasted time. I can stay in a funk for months or weeks at a time, or I can stay in it for only hours or minutes. Since the training I have managed my moods and handled my mistakes more responsibly.

"I laugh more at myself and I get a kick out of things I do. I don't take myself as seriously. And I don't take other people's feedback about me as seriously. If someone says something about me now, I can more easily understand why they would feel that way. No one likes negative feedback, and the ability to deal with it is a good thing. You can be defensive, but that doesn't resolve anything. I take responsibility for the way they feel as opposed to saying, 'Well, you're full of it.' It isn't false for them—it really is the way they feel. I take it upon myself to improve the relationship. I came to a kind of awareness about why people say what they say about me through the experiences I had in the training.

"I did a lot of soul-searching in the training. Questions like, 'Why am I on the planet?' 'What's my purpose in life?' 'What is success, really?' I got clear that one of my purposes is to be a good father and example to my children. After my first wife and I divorced, my two kids were in Arizona and I was in California. I used to talk to them on the phone and visit them often. I was a pretty decent absentee father; however, the direct experience of raising my kids on a daily basis was different than visiting Phoenix once a month and calling two or three times a week. I really cheated myself out of the experience of being a full-time father. Now, I am remarried and my wife and I have two terrific kids. They are a very special part of my life.

"The courses had a profound effect on my relationship with my own parents. I let go of a lot of the anxieties that I had about that relationship. After the training I shared with them some of the things that had been bothering me for almost forty years. We all cried together at breakfast one morning. When we talk on the phone to each other now oftentimes we say 'I love you.' We never said that before. That relationship improved dramatically largely, or solely, because during and after the trainings I got some things out of the way that had been bothering me for thirty-odd years.

"The Basic Course was the single, biggest thing I did to improve my communication skills, allowing me to listen and speak at a different level than I was capable of beforehand. I had taken negotiating courses, management courses, and so forth, before. Then, what Lifespring did was enable me to internalize all the concepts. It caused me to communicate far more effectively than I had before. I was listening better and I was communicating from a deeper place inside myself.

"The training was a real eye-opener. I had a joyous experience of myself. The processes were enlightening. I started realizing that I had a lot of good inside of me, but that my methods weren't necessarily consistent with what I was feeling inside. Since the training, my life has been about bringing my actions in line with what I feel is genuinely important."

Choice

16

A favorite topic of the "human potential" or pop psychology movement is choice. Many people seem to think that using the word "choice" makes them responsible, casual, enlightened people. "Choice" has become one of the buzz-words of the new age. Unfortunately, the meaningful substance of choice has nothing to do with the jargon. Acknowledging that you have chosen, if it is authentic for you, can empower you to both be more effective and to have peace of mind.

DO WE REALLY HAVE FREE CHOICE?

What is choice? And how valid is it to claim that we have free choice in many of life's situations?

If you get punched in the stomach, do you think you have a choice about feeling pain? When you laugh, do you make a choice to be happy, or does it just seem to take you over?

Earlier, we looked at how the time, place, and circumstances to which we are "thrown" at birth place boundaries on the possibilities available to us. Even our structure of interpretation is determined to a degree by how we are situated in the world. Not only are our physical options constrained, but also our intellectual, behavioral, and experiential options are at least partially determined by our personal history.

To choose is defined as to select freely after consideration. But, how free are you to select? Maybe your freedom to choose is not as absolute as some philosophies suggest. As we've said, the options that are actually available to you depend, in part, on your history. Further, your options also depend on the choices you have already made throughout your life. Some people hold the belief that you have chosen everything in your life, including your parents, your gender, the death of loved ones, your own illnesses, and so on. Others believe that human beings actually have no choice at all, that we are merely playing out a predestined script. Either of those possibilities may exist, but I suggest yet another proposition.

Forget how your life got to be the way it is. How you handle it in this moment is what we are concerned with. Your life is the way it is now, period. So now what? What is your stand about who you are and what you are becoming? Choice may or may not allow you control over the circumstances of life, but inasmuch as you can choose your interpretations and the context from which you participate in life, choice can influence your effectiveness and the quality of your experience.

HAVE TO / CHOOSE TO

Let's look at choice in a very practical framework. Think of something you don't like to do, but you do because you must (e.g., pay taxes, work, cook dinner every night for your family, spend time with your in-laws, etc.). Now, think of all the consequences you would pay if you did not do it, including the emotional prices. Carry the scenario out to its extreme. For instance, you have to work because if you didn't, you would not have enough money to support yourself; if you didn't have enough money to support yourself, you would feel like a failure; if you felt like a failure, you would feel sorry for yourself; if you felt sorry for yourself, you would hate yourself; if you hated yourself, you would withdraw from your friends and family; if you shut out your friends and family, you would feel totally alone. . . . You could take this in many directions. It may even seem silly, but exploring the deeper causes for your actions, particularly those which you consider obligatory, is a key to shifting your experience. Pick something in your life that you have to do even though you don't like doing it, and carry the consequences of not doing it to the deepest bottom line for you.

Based on the fact that you *are* doing whatever you selected as your "have to," it is obvious that you would rather do it than pay the consequences of not doing it. The operative word in the last sentence is *rather*. Rather implies choice. But, come on—what kind of a choice is that? To do unsatisfying work or to feel totally alone?! Somehow the choice between those two options doesn't instill a terrific sense of freedom.

Maybe freedom shows up in a different way. Maybe it has to do with how you *interpret* your choices, whether you declare they are things you "have" to do, or things you "choose" to do. Who knows whether human beings have free choice, partial choice, or no choice at all? What we do know is that your interpretation of choice will definitely influence your participation in your life and, in so doing, will increase your effectiveness and satisfaction.

I am not suggesting a semantic adjustment. Merely using the appropriate jargon obviously won't make a difference in your experience of life. Although the language you use is a valuable clue about your attitudes, the qualitative shift from "have to" to "choose to" goes far beyond your vocabulary. Have you ever noticed that you can do something once and it's a "have to," but the same thing another time is a "want to?" The difference isn't in your words. The same person can at different times have two different perspectives on the same choice—both totally opposed, yet equally authentic. Your interpretation of your choices can affect not only your experience of life, but your effectiveness too.

Look at those things that you "have to" do, but aren't thrilled about. Some examples may include: working, going to school, managing your finances, staying informed about what is happening in the world, going to social functions for work, staying physically fit. Isn't it ironic that the very things in life that are potentially the most rewarding are so commonly perceived as unpleasant duties and obligations?

What experiences accompany feeling duty bound and obligated? Guilt, anger, worry, anxiety, self-pity, suffering, frustration, confusion, boredom, feeling trapped, tiredness, worthlessness, martyrdom, pain, burden, fear, and depression, to name a few. These experiences are likely to be generated from a sense of having lost freedom, individuality, or control of your own life; and losing control means facing the possibility of not looking good. When you interpret something as a "have to," you automatically experience the negative feelings that correspond with that interpretation. This brings us back to the notion of *context*. Remember, just as ferns can't grow in the desert, you can't experience freedom if you are operating from a context of duty and obligation.

Part of shifting the context of "have to" to one of choice is to understand what the payoffs are for the negative feelings associated with the "have to" interpretation. What is the personal payoff for being depressed, frustrated, angry, resentful, guilty, and so on? One type of payoff is attention; you may get recognition, approval, sympathy, reassurance, and appreciation for doing things that, based on the negative emotional impact you exhibit, *must* require sacrifice on your part. Another type of payoff for having those negative feelings is that they provide you excuses; you can use them to justify yourself for slacking off, not risking, failing, being unaccountable, and breaking your word. For instance, how can anyone expect you to perform your best at work when you are so angry at your boss; or depressed about the fight you had with your girlfriend or boyfriend; or worried about whether your daughter makes it in cheerleader tryouts; or frustrated about your car breaking down on the way to work; or . . . ? A third kind of payoff is the power those negative emotions give you over others; you have leverage to manipulate and control others, you can deceive others, and you can maintain your image of being a great person even when you are behaving irresponsibly. For example, when you break your word with somebody, doesn't feeling really guilty about it show that you are really a good person in spite of your actions? Doesn't being angry at someone often get him or her to do what you want, or to take responsibility that belongs to you? Finally, these negative feelings protect you; your beliefs are reinforced, your actions are justified whether they are productive or not, and you have reason to avoid taking action. In general, you get to be right. For instance, being resentful when your boyfriend dumps you reinforces your belief that men can't be trusted. Or, being angry when your girlfriend dumps you for another man reinforces your belief that you can't live up to a woman's expectations. If you forget to do something you said you would do, you are justified by your confusion about the plans. As you can see, there are numerous permutations of the payoffs of the "have to" structure of interpretation. At the bottom of it all, *no matter what happens,* the fault and the solution is always outside of you, and *no matter what you do,* you come out seeming to smell like a rose.

Examine the patterns in your life. Write your thoughts in your journal.

- What aspects of your life do you hold as 'have tos'?
- What would the consequences be if you did not do those things? Carry them out to the extreme, even though it may seem ridiculous.
- Is it true that you would rather do whatever it is than pay the prices of not doing it?
- What are the negative feelings or experiences that you get from feeling duty-bound and obligated?
- What are the payoffs you receive from those feelings?

What brings about the negative feelings? Most often they result from comparing what is with what you think *should* be. Take resentment, for example. One source of resentment is a discrepancy between your expectations of someone and their actions. On the down side, this person has power over you. To the degree that you focus on what you resent about them and about how they are a problem for you, your freedom is limited—your energy is siphoned off to wishing they were different than they are. Further, by placing blame for your problems on someone else, you cramp your own ability to solve the problems. You tend to react rather than initiate, and collect evidence to prove how terrible they are rather than take responsibility for yourself. You have given someone else the responsibility for your experience of life. This person may or may not be aware of your resentment and use it to their own ends, but either way you have abdicated control over your own experience and actions. Do you ever notice that usually, although you may think you can somehow change someone with your resentment, your attitude only reinforces or worsens the behavior that you are resisting? On the up side, however, there are definitely payoffs to resentment. As we have said, by holding on to your resentment, you can blame someone or something outside of yourself, and you have a justification for not taking responsibility yourself. Holding on to your idea of the way things "should be" instead of surrendering to the way they are allows you to rationalize not taking action.

Regardless of whether or not we choose what happens in our lives, interpreting events that way gives you a freedom that the "have to" interpretation kills.

Try this exercise in your journal to further your inquiry about choice.

- Begin to look at the 'have tos' in your life as 'choose tos.'
- What do you have to be willing to be wrong about in order to change your interpretation from 'have to' to 'choose to?'
- What results from the new interpretation?
- Over the next 24 hours, say 'I choose to,' 'I want to,' or 'I get to' when you would normally say 'I have to.' It may only be a semantic change at first, but notice how it shifts your experience.

COMPARISON

Think of some of the times when you either made a "wrong" choice, or did not make the best choice you could have. Notice how the only way you can assess a choice as being the wrong choice is to compare it with another choice, one that you did not make. We automatically judge our choices based on some standard that we have made up about how we think something *should* have turned out. Maybe an example will clarify this pattern.

Imagine this. You are James Bond. You are trapped in a small room with no doors, no windows, no openings at all. Suddenly, the ceiling draws back to reveal a threatening panel of nails—long, sharp, and pointing down at you. The room starts to close in on you. The nails inch their way toward your head, and the space around you diminishes as the room slowly shrinks. Then, you notice two pits at the edge of the room. Each pit has a sign next to it. One sign says "Raw sewage—4 ft." The other sign says "Raw sewage—8 ft." So, you have some choices. The first choice is to stay where you are, be impaled by a panel of nails, and squished beyond recognition. Or you could jump into one of the pits. You decide to jump. Now you have another choice—which pit? Being no dummy, you choose the pit with four feet of raw sewage. You close your eyes, hold your nose, and you jump just as the walls slam together above you.

When you land, your first thought is something like: "Ugh, this stinks!" Now, is there a likelihood you might think something like: "This is great—only four feet of raw sewage instead of eight feet!"? Probably not, but think about it. Didn't you make the best choices available to you at each moment? Yes. Then why are you upset about being in four feet of raw sewage? Because you are comparing it with something else—"I should be on the beach in Maui," or "This should be rose water"—as though the beach on Maui, or a rose water bath were available choices. You are comparing your choices with options that weren't available at the time you made your decision to jump. Given the circumstances you were facing, you made the best possible choices at each point along the way.

That story is a metaphor which can apply to other choices you have made. Regarding *all* the choices you have made, don't you think that if there were better choices available, you would have made them?

Take the Prince and Princess Charming myths. Princess Charming is: gorgeous (but only has eyes for you), smart (but not smarter than you), rich (but doesn't earn more than you); she loves sports, is a sizzling lover (and is interested twenty-four hours a day), anticipates and takes care of your every desire (but isn't clingy or a doormat), loves to clean up after you, loves it when you go out drinking with the boys (but doesn't go out with the girls so she can always be at home with you), is a great cook and a fabulous mother, looks great when she wakes up in the morning, isn't the slightest bit demanding (but is fervently appreciative of everything you do for her), thinks you are the sexiest man alive, and so on.

And let's be fair, women. How is Prince Charming? He's sensitive and gentle (but not a wimp), caring, a hunk (but doesn't even notice all the other women drooling over him), rich (and what he doesn't already spend on you, you may spend as you like), sexy (but is never interested unless you are), smart (but not condescending), giving (you never have to ask for what you want, he just instinctively knows); he would never look at another woman, shares equally in all household responsibilities, is the model father, always asks your opinion before making decisions, loves to talk about whatever is on your mind, would move in a second if your career required it, and so forth. Do Prince and Princess Charming exist? If they did, wouldn't you be in a relationship with him or her? Instead, there you are stuck with that slob!

And what about Career Charming? It is . . . challenging and creative, pays you an enormous salary; your schedule is flexible; people there listen to you and respect your opinion; you have an unlimited expense account, travel only to the most exciting cities, and only first class. Again, don't you think if that job were an available option, you'd be doing it? Then there are Kids Charming, Car Charming, House Charming, Parents Charming, and Body Charming.

Thanks to Madison Avenue we are all conditioned to think that life should be one climax after another—Life Charming. Everything you do should be exciting, fulfilling, enriching. Every moment should be titillating, better than the moment before it. The problem with this is that, in reality, most of life consists of plateaus, not peak experiences one after another. When life isn't a thrill a minute, we compare it with the thrills we're not having (and that are not available to us anyway). Comparison is thus a source of tremendous unnecessary dissatisfaction, and can lead us to abandon or resent commitments that hold rich possibilities.

YOUR FREEDOM TO CHOOSE

Are you supposed to resign yourself to live in four feet of raw sewage —and to love every minute of it? It depends on your interpretation. First of all, it is silly and useless to judge the choices you have made against alternatives that were not available to begin with. Second, there is more freedom to take effective action if you accept and take full responsibility for the choices you have made rather than compare them to some fantasy. Third, the quality of your experience of life depends on *your interpretations*. Why would you choose an interpretation that traps you in an endless cycle of regrets? There will always be someone richer, smarter, faster than you; and a better spouse, job, house than yours. Or will there? You are only dealing with your interpretations of those things. It isn't a "fact" that your wife is a nag, your husband is lazy, or your job is frustrating—it is your interpretation. Comparison is a mental exercise that wastes time and energy. Fourth, you cannot always control the circumstances that show up in your life or the options available to you. Given that, the most constructive way to look at choice is to manage your interpretations and your level of participation, *regardless* of the circumstances.

Rather than try to maneuver yourself into ideal situations, choose a context that serves you in *any* situation. Rather than avoid tough decisions and uncomfortable situations, work on clarifying what is really important to you. When you are clear about what is worth taking a stand about, you have solid ground on which to base your choices. Rather than analyze or regret your choice of spouse, career, or home (or any past decisions), look instead at what you are committed to accomplishing in each of those areas now. *So what* if things aren't the way you want them to be. The relevant questions to ask yourself are: "What's next?" and "What am *I* going to do about this?"

In examining the questions below, look at what possibilities would be available to you if you shifted your context to one of choice in those areas where it is now duty and obligation and comparison. Use your journal to record your thoughts.

- To what people or ideals do you most commonly compare yourself?
- What 'negative' judgments do you have about yourself, your job, spouse, co-workers, kids? How do those judgments hinder your own effectiveness? Is it possible that your judgments even hinder *their* effectiveness?
- List the ways in which you resist making choices, or try to second-guess the future in order to make the 'best' choice?
- What past choices do you regret? What is your payoff for regretting those choices?
- Are you open to the possibility that you have a choice about your interpretation, that you have control over the context that governs your attitudes and actions?
- How would your life be affected if you shifted to a 100 percent 'choose to' interpretation?

17

Linda Rosso

GRADUATE PROFILE

When Linda Rosso decided to take the Lifespring Basic Training in New York City in 1982, her life was, to use her word, wonderful. "I didn't really have to do anything about it. I got into the right college, and had the right grades, and looked the right way, and lived in the right neighborhood, and all that. I always 'looked' really good. I had prestigious jobs making the right amount of money, wore the right clothes, and so forth. But, I realized that I was making very passive choices. I was very conscious of what I *didn't* want, but I was probably less conscious of what I *did* want. I would postpone making choices. I found myself unconsciously drifting into commitments, turning provisional choices into commitments.

"I was 25 when I first heard about Lifespring through a friend. He was a very social, outgoing, gregarious person. We used to go out after work all the time—we'd go to these chic little bars on Madison Avenue. We'd be there with each other, but we'd be scoping the whole place out, checking out who's here, who's there. This one particular time we went out was very different. He was talking about himself in a very different way. I wondered what was going on. He was so peaceful and attentive, and more sincere than I'd ever seen him before. I got a sense that the course was something very powerful."

About the Basic Training, Linda says: "It was time I took time for myself to observe firsthand how I behave in my life and, at the same time, start doing something about it. It's not like taking a seminar at work in effective time management. There's something special about the training in that while I was observing myself I was also doing something about myself. I got a chance to practice what I'd just noticed and correct it in a very nonthreatening arena. For instance, I had this realization that I didn't always communicate very clearly, and people didn't always understand what I said. Well, right then and there in the training I had an opportunity with a group of people to practice meaning what I said and saying what I meant."

Out of what she observed in herself and experienced about how she was in the world, Linda began to participate more proactively in her life. "I realized that I have a vote in what I am committed to. Exercising that voting power has enabled me to make major life decisions affecting marriage, motherhood, home, and career that I probably wouldn't have made prior to the trainings."

One of Linda's discoveries had to do with her relationships with people and, in particular, with men. It began when her partner for one of the exercises on Saturday morning started flirting with her after the exercise was over. It bothered her so much that she started examining her reaction. "I started looking at the rules and games I made up about men who act this way with me. For example, if I was on a date with a guy and he'd ask me if I had ever been a model, I decided he wasn't worth going out with because he was just interested in what I looked like. I'm somewhat shy in social situations anyway, but I was being perceived as very aloof. So the combination of my reaction to being complimented on my appearance and my shyness, which came across as aloofness, was a deadly mixture.

"I realized that I wasn't being fair to other people because I was just assuming right away that they were judging the book by its cover. But I wasn't doing anything to invite them in. The analogy I'd use is this: It's Christmas morning and there are all these packages under the tree. I would be this really wonderfully wrapped package, with this great bow on it, and people would be drawn to it. It's a very under-stated package, mind you. Understated, but desirable. In the training I realized what I'd let people do; I'd let people pick up the package and shake it, but there was no way that bow was coming untied. I realized in the training that I had to take the ribbons off and loosen the edges of the paper. Since the training, I have applied this discovery in my life. Now that I take initiative, people respond to me like they never did before.

"I was taking more responsibility for my life. I had always been a big dawdler, mostly because I didn't see any real reason to get so excited about doing something. Before doing the trainings, I was in that sort of passive mode. Once I got into something, I'd get very passionate about it, but I never questioned what my aspirations were. I operated on the assumption that everything was just going to hap-pen. Because it always did. After the trainings, and even now, six years later, I notice that I intervene instead of just sitting back. I get really involved in things rather than just spinning tops all around me. Since the training, things are happening faster. I am getting more done. I'll have ten things going at one time. Sometimes it causes stress, but it is a very positive stress. I feel that the more I am doing, the more I can do. I feel much more like a participant than an observer.

"Although I would have predicted that things were simpler before the trainings when I was just observing, actually it is simpler now that I'm involved in directing my life. I'm not constantly worrying about how things are going or what other people are going to think. I used to analyze things to death. Whenever the time came to make a choice about something major, I would go through excruciating analysis and I would ask everybody their advice. I probably didn't hear any of it, but I would just complicate things by not trusting my own instincts. I was always consulting other people about the right thing to do. That caused a lot more stress because it was a way of being even less in-volved in my life—I was sort of turning it over to other people. Being involved in my life and making my own decisions and sticking with them is much more relaxing."

Linda, now thirty-two, is pregnant with her first child. She got married about two years ago and moved to California with her husband. "The first couple of months of my pregnancy, I couldn't stand not being in charge of what was happening with my body. I felt like I had an alien living inside of me that was taking charge of my life. I really did not like it. Then something shifted. I don't know quite when it happened or what it was, but I realized, 'Oh, what the hell. This is just going to happen. I might as well go along with it.' So now I'm just more relaxed about everything. It's a very different feeling than just unconsciously drifting through the experience. I have a lot more trust in myself about how things are going to turn out."

Linda's life has changed a lot since she did the Lifespring trainings, particularly in the last two years. "I have a house in the suburbs and a Volvo station wagon, mind you. My life has dramatically changed in two years. Very dramatically. My life may have taken a very different path had I not done the trainings. I know that many of the people whom I was on a par with, keeping pace with—my friends in New York—their lives have evolved in a completely different way. A lot of the change for me has to do with being in the relationship I'm in now. Getting married and having a partner to do things with gives me a foundation. Had I not created this relationship, my life would probably still be very much career driven, working very hard, living in the city, being seen with the right people. Those would be the things that would be more important. If I hadn't done the training, I probably wouldn't have allowed a relationship like this to happen.

"The biggest effect the training had was on my self-concept. Without that the other things wouldn't have shifted. The training affected my sense of security with myself. I always knew I was doing the right thing. I would listen to all these other people, but I did what I wanted anyway. I just had to get other people's opinions and feedback, and I had to test out my thesis on a number of people. I don't do that anymore. I trust myself and I trust that my decisions are right for me. I don't just fall into provisional choices that may not be best for me. I trust myself to make choices and to participate fully in my life."

The Stand for Responsibility

18

"If not for the IRS, I'd have enough money to do the things I want to do." "I'm so busy handling things for my kids, I don't have any time for myself." "Work would be much smoother if my boss weren't so disorganized." "The traffic keeps making me late." "As soon as my husband/wife can spend more time with me, our marriage will start working better." "I was just in the wrong place at the wrong time." "If only I'd gotten my Ph.D. I would really be successful." "If my husband would help more around the house, I wouldn't be so tired and stressed all the time." "If my wife would stop nagging me, I'd be able to relax a little bit." "If it weren't for a couple of dedicated teachers, I never would have made it through school on my own." "Nobody recognizes my contribution at the office because my co-worker grabs all the credit." "It was just a twist of fate, an accident waiting to happen." "My parents were never there for me, so now I have a hard time asking people for support." "If I were married, I would feel so much more complete."

This chapter is about exploring your willingness to be responsible and declaring a new stand about responsibility. Your outlook on responsibility influences how you interpret the facts of reality. You will be looking at responsibility on two separate levels. First, you'll examine your attitudes about responsibility and how they make up the background that determines your generalized worldview. You'll see that your disposition to behave certain ways emerges from that background. Second, you will see how you interpret your own accountability in specific events. Taking a stand for being 100 percent responsible shifts your relationship with yourself and the rest of the world, opening new possibilities for effective behavior.

I will be using the words responsibility and accountability interchangeably. Those words refer to a structure of interpretation by which you declare that you are fully the cause of what happens in your life—including your thoughts, feelings, interpretations, actions, *and* the resulting events. My assertion is that assuming full responsibility allows you to be the most effective, powerful, and creative in the face of all circumstances.

Two distinct and mutually exclusive structures of interpretation are: the victim interpretation and the responsible interpretation. The characteristics of each permeate both your worldview and your specific behavior. To take a meaningful and potent stand for responsibility you must first understand the distinctions of each domain.

THE VICTIM

Someone or something is always doing things to victims or forcing them to do things against their better judgment or will. They are at the mercy of circumstances, and circumstances are always beyond their control. The victim is the good guy, and "it" or "they" are the bad guys. A lot in the victim's life is out of his or her control, and problems or breakdowns are not their fault. Sometimes they even credit someone or something else with their accomplishments. The victim's interpretation is one by which his or her actions and feelings are determined by outside agents.

To operate as a victim, one need not necessarily have been victimized by anything or anyone specific. Generally, victims perceive the world as an opponent they are up against, or, at best, a headache they have to put up with. Themes of the victim's experience are hope, regret, resignation, and the need to explain. Victims go through life reacting, coping, blaming, and justifying; events and circumstances "have" them.

Telling a story of a specific situation in which you actually have been victimized (i.e., having your car or house broken into, being raped, being left by a spouse, having someone close to you die, etc.) evokes a consistent range of moods and behaviors. For example, you will tend to feel and act helpless, hurt, bitter, out of control, resentful, righteous, self-pitying, betrayed, abused, cheated, angry. What are the odds that these moods and behaviors are likely to promote effectiveness and breakthrough?

The victim is a conspirator in his or her victimhood, acting covertly to set up conditions that make it seem like outside agents have control over his or her actions and experience. Victims participate in their own victimhood—at some level they are only pretending to be victimized. We all know people who seem to be constantly telling dramatic stories of how they were "done to." Often, we are not surprised when something bad happens to those people; it is typical of how that person's life works. There are times when life truly serves you a bad deal, but the way a victim responds attracts or magnifies the drama. The victim has a stake in his or her victimhood and constructs the flow of his or her life to perpetuate it.

What is the payoff for being a victim? First, you get justification for not taking action. Since there's nothing you can do about anything anyway, any proactive steps you take would be futile. The victim would rather deal with the consequences of *not* acting than face the responsibility of taking initiative. This is the person who whines and complains about everything that is preventing him or her from having the good things in life. Not all victims whine, of course. Some are very stoic about it. Some just can't understand why their lives aren't working out. Really hip victims take all kinds of awareness seminars, and then explain to you why their lives aren't working, but don't seem "to be able" to do anything about it. Unlike people who are clear about their commitments and are willing to pay some prices in the short run to manifest their dreams in the long run, victims are often unclear about where they are headed, simply reacting to whatever comes up. Of course, both people will pay prices and reap rewards. One price that responsible people pay is that they must be willing to expend the energy and time to follow through on their ideas, and they risk making mistakes. One of the "rewards" you get when you play the victim is that you can sit back and let life happen to you, saving the time, energy, and emotional risk of taking your own initiative.

A second payoff for being a victim is that you get to maintain your image regardless of the circumstances. Since you didn't have anything to do with what happened, you don't need to worry about not looking good because of it. Victims always have a scapegoat and several layers of excuses that buffer them from the source of any problem. It is dangerous to be around a victim because you run the risk of being the one on whom he or she places the blame for a problem or the responsibility for a solution. For a victim, it is unacceptable and unbearable to make mistakes, whereas in a responsible context, mistakes are understood to be part of the game. The preservation of a victim's self-image depends on interpreting reality in a way that finds him or her blameless. Thus, the victim's perception of reality is often warped to a degree that hinders his or her capacity to act effectively. Further, victims can't be counted on to make significant contributions toward resolving breakdowns—especially if *their* mistake is part of the problem—since they are so consumed with looking good in the eyes of themselves and others.

Finally, in being a victim you gain leverage with which to manipulate and control others. You may get others' sympathy, their help, and, best of all, the support you get from them validates that you were victimized. There is a sense of community about victimhood in our culture; we readily accept our own and other people's victim stories.

The culture in general and we as individuals do each other a great disservice when we support each other's victim stories. Compared with a responsible interpretation of life, the victim interpretation inhibits your ability to take initiative and be creative. A key distinction about the responsible structure of interpretation that enables effective action is that you are willing to tell the truth in order to move forward, even if it means admitting to being less than perfect. In a responsible framework, your ego needs are subordinate to the accomplishment of your commitments. Conversely, the victim abdicates responsibility and is willing to sacrifice the final result in an ego-driven effort to look good. The strategy required to look good can sabotage the ultimate success of the victim's projects. There are a million ways in which this is evident in the world. One typical example is when someone makes a mistake in business and discovers it in time to rectify it, but conceals his or her discovery because it would be self-incriminating, and takes the victim stance instead—making it seem that the outcome of the project was out of his or her control. Hence, the cover-up that is intended to protect that individual's reputation damages his or her short-term and long-term results. Had this person been willing to admit the mistake as soon as he or she discovered it, there would have been the opportunity to intervene and solve the problem rather than put all energy into dodging blame. Now, of course this is an obvious distinction in theory, but it isn't that easy to live by. Our relationships are set up to tolerate self-aggrandizement at the expense of the greater good. The price of admitting your mistakes makes the victim role attractive in many ways. The more firmly we as a culture, and as individuals, accommodate the victim context and make people pay for being responsible, the less possibility for effective, committed action.

Victim stories rationalize the present based on a past that was out of their control and thus set up a future that is also beyond their control. Since there was nothing they could do about "it" before, what can they do about it now or in the future? And if there was nothing they could do about "that," then there probably isn't much they can really do about *anything*. Thus, in being victims in the present, individuals set up their future alibis.

Be candid about your tendencies to be a victim and write your responses in your journal.

- On what specific occasions have you actually been victimized?
- On what or whom do you most often place blame when things don't turn out?
- Describe how you behave when you are victimized.
- What do you get out of taking the victim stance?

RESPONSIBILITY

People who operate in a context of responsibility, on the other hand, declare that they are accountable for their interpretations and behavior. Caring mainly about the ultimate success of their projects, they are oriented to action and correction rather than explanation and self-protection. They don't spend a lot of energy estimating how things got to be the way they are, but rather focus on effective action. They are more concerned with having a project work than with the reasons why it won't.

This is not to imply that victims are not concerned with having their projects work—they are. In fact, being a victim is often precisely how they *get* their projects to turn out; they manage projects by locating both problems and solutions outside of themselves. In the responsible structure of interpretation, one, instead, looks to oneself as the source of all aspects of the project. The victim sees peoples' roles in terms of credit and blame, the responsible person in terms of what works and what does not work.

When you are responsible, you voice few psychological assessments, focusing instead on what action will further your project or relationship. You are able, willing, and striving to tell the truth about what you did and didn't do. You are not as concerned with looking good as you are with having life *work*.

Real responsibility is not to be confused with blame, credit, obligation, or duty. Acting from a context of responsibility, you are concerned with the facts inasmuch as they bear on your next actions, not on whether they give you credit or blame. A stand of responsibility does not signify restrictive ties, but freedom to act. When you operate out of a stand of responsibility, you are *empowered* by being the source of your results, not intimidated or weighed down by it.

Take a story about a time when you were victimized and tell it instead as though you were actually responsible for what happened. Even if you don't believe it yourself, pretend that you were responsible and build a case to support that point of view. Imagine you have to convince someone of your responsibility even if you don't see it that way yourself. Experiment with a responsible interpretation of the same facts which before now you have interpreted from the point of view of a victim.

Do you notice a difference in your experience even when you are just pretending to look at the situation from a responsible point of view? Typical moods and behaviors generated from a responsible context are freedom, choice, control, powerfulness, honesty, peacefulness, ease, relief—all conducive to effective action and possibility.

You may pay prices when you live life responsibly. For one thing, you have to give up all the goodies you got from being a victim: the reasons not to take action; the protection of your image; the leverage with which to manipulate others, get their sympathy, and get them to handle things for you. You risk standing alone, and even take hostility from others who may not be willing to live on the edge, who may prefer the conspiracy, comfort, and pain of victimhood.

People living in the different frameworks of victim and responsibility may agree on the facts of a situation, but their interpretations of the causes, effects, and appropriate responses will be different. How you interpret and participate in events tends to generate evidence supporting your beliefs. Your interpretations have a cyclic relationship with your actions, each reinforcing and regenerating the other.

Are you, in fact, responsible for absolutely everything in your life? Are you responsible for nothing? Or are you responsible in certain situations, but not in others? If the answer to the last question is yes, then how do you discern when you are responsible and when you aren't? If you look at it one way, human beings are ultimate victims— you didn't have a choice about being born, you aren't responsible for being male or female, Catholic or Jewish, blue eyed or brown eyed, tall or short, American or Chinese. You are completely molded by your history, culture, and language. There are external circumstances that are clearly beyond your control: the weather, natural disasters, other peoples' actions, and so on. You are powerless over all that has gone before you, and powerless over much of the physical universe.

In a court of law you hear two entirely different interpretations of the exact same facts. The legal process is designed to steer our interpretations of the facts toward a conclusion that is valid according to the law. In life, however, there is no system for judging responsibility. Being responsible or being a victim is a question of interpretation, not of fact. Being responsible in your own life takes a willingness to jump in and take a stand about it, without having evidence, formulas or guarantees.

I invite you to explore the possibilities for you in taking a stand for responsibility in your life.

TAKING A STAND FOR RESPONSIBILITY

Why take a stand for responsibility if a victim stand is easier, has a whole bunch of neat under-the-table benefits, and doesn't require you to oppose the already strong cultural drift of victimhood? The answer to that lies in another question: What are you committed to getting accomplished? If your intention is to become more effective, the only place worth looking is at your own responsibility.

While it may be true that you have played the victim in certain situations, hanging on to those stories can set the stage for future events in your life for a long time. Unless you face up to your past responsibly, it will continue to run you.

What can you do about it when you really seem to have been victimized? You don't have control over many aspects of life. But you do have control over your interpretations. You do have control of how events and people influence your attitudes and behaviors. You do have control over your response to the conditions and events in your life.

Responsibility is a stand you take about life—you take life on as a responsible agent and that's how you look at the world. You operate *as if* you were responsible for everything, including those things over which you may not have control.

When you take absolute responsibility for how things are, you can begin to act more effectively because you require from yourself the resources that the victim can only hope to get from outside him- or herself. The victim's interpretations are unreliable, at best, since they are, by nature, colored by self-serving explanations and justifications. When you are willing to take responsibility for what isn't working as well as what is (not confusing responsibility with blame), you process information and facts differently, without a personal investment in how they reflect on you. You end up with more accurate data. You, therefore, have a solid background from which to take effective action.

Operating responsibly, you participate with other people out of a commitment to intervention and mutual accomplishment. For victims, relationships include avoiding domination, not getting hurt, getting what they think they deserve, getting credit, assigning blame, and other forms of manipulation. From a stand for responsibility, your relationships with other people shift as you become more concerned with contributing to them in a way that makes a substantive difference than with what they can do to or for you. A stand for responsibility is the throttle of effective intervention.

To begin to unfold the distinctions of a stand for responsibility, and to clarify where *you* stand about it, ask yourself these questions in your next journal entry.

- When you told your victim story as if you were responsible (*not* to blame) for the turn of events, what was your experience of that event? How was that experience different from when you told the story as a sincere victim?
- What are your interactions with others like when you see yourself as a victim? What possibilities are opened and closed?
- What are your interactions with others like when you see *them* as victims? What possibilities are opened and closed?
- If you were to take an absolute stand for responsibility, in what situations and relationships might new possibilities open up? What actions would you take that you haven't taken so far?
- If you were to take an absolute stand for responsibility, you might experience some uncomfortableness when you confront the situations and relationships in which you formerly played the victim. Are you willing to be uncomfortable for the sake of standing for responsibility?
- Take a stand for absolute responsibility for one week whether or not you understand it or agree with it. Do you accept this request? If you make this promise, what specific actions will you take immediately to assist you to shift your interpretations and behavior?

How exactly do you take a stand for responsibility? Although there are indicators, there are no rules to follow and no litmus tests to measure your responsibility. You stand for responsibility by declaration. Through experience you can begin to reveal its nature and its value for yourself. It is analogous to being coached in a sport. If your tennis coach tells you to hit the ball in a particular way, you will only get how it works when you begin hitting the ball that way yourself. You know that the goal is to be a more effective tennis player, but must count on your coach to guide you in the process. Similarly, you can listen to theories and stories about responsibility all you want, but you must start taking action even before it makes sense to you—you will only begin to grasp the meaning of it when you actually shift your own practices. As you consistently interpret situations as the responsible agent, you will become increasingly disposed to behaving responsibly and effectively. The stand for responsibility validates and reinforces itself.

THE LANGUAGE OF A STAND FOR RESPONSIBILITY

The language with which you speak about yourself and your life reflects and reinforces your stand about anything; responsibility, choice, concern for others, and so on. Our words, phrases, intonation, and body language are clues to the general context from which we operate. People who consistently say things like "I would have, but . . ." "I tried to . . ." "If only . . ." "If not for . . ." "I wish . . ." "I'll try . . ." and "I hope I can . . ." expose a tendency toward the victim attitude. On the other hand, language like "I promise . . ." "I will . . ." and "I didn't . . ." expose a tendency toward and attitude of responsibility. The power of the spoken word to bring forth reality cannot be understated.

In your process of transformation, a deliberate and rigorous shift in your use of the language and in your practices will assist you to embody the subtle aspects of responsibility and all other shifts you make in this work. When explaining why something turned out the way it did, begin your sentence with "I" rather than with "they," "he," "she," or "it." Practice publicly acknowledging your role in events, both when you are effective and when you make mistakes. When you encounter breakdowns, ask yourself questions like "What do I need to do to correct this?" "Whose assistance do I need to request to resolve this?" "Who else needs to know this so their projects won't be jeopardized?"

YOU'RE ON YOUR OWN

A stand for responsibility belongs to you alone. Shared responsibility is an oxymoron—like jumbo shrimp, pretty ugly, and Internal Revenue Service. You can participate with others who also operate in a context of responsibility, but you can't share responsibility in common with others. Jean-Paul Sartre expressed this eloquently: "Man can will nothing unless he has first understood that he must count on no one but himself; that he is alone, abandoned on earth in the midst of his infinite responsibilities, without help, with no other aim than the one he sets himself, with no other destiny than the one he forges for himself on this earth."

Debbie Stamper

19

GRADUATE PROFILE

Debbie Stamper calls vulnerability "the V word." I mention the word vulnerability and tears come to my eyes. It's the thing I have the most resistance to.

"I was always critical and judgmental of others. I put on a big show that I had it all together. I found out that a lot of people were afraid to approach me. I was always real nice, and I'd speak to people, but I'd really be saying, 'Don't come any closer than this!' It was all tied up in my image, what I thought I was supposed to be, and the way I wanted to appear to other people. Again, the word vulnerable comes up—not to show anybody that I'm vulnerable and that I need other people.

"I remember the first night of the Basic Training I was so bored. I couldn't believe the other participants were not getting the point about the Ground Rules. I was so arrogant, I didn't think I could spend five days with those people.

"Other people experienced me as arrogant, too. I got feedback that when I was not being vulnerable, people experienced me as cold, calculating, manipulative. My greatest fear is to appear that way. I thought I was supposed to be perfect. Perfect is a word I really loved. It was the training that allowed me to just surrender to the softer side of me and to recognize that it's okay. I don't have to be strong and independent and assertive all the time.

Several times Debbie mentioned the significance of discovering that she needed people, so we explored what that means to her. "Well, I've never really considered myself a loner, but I do spend tons of time by myself. I think I've allowed a lot of people to come in and out of my life. But I've allowed them to leave without really telling them how much they've meant to me and what they contributed to me. Saying 'I love you' has always been a real hard thing for me to get out of my mouth. I could never say 'You really do mean a lot to me.' In that respect I think I wasn't open about my feelings. Again, it goes back to honest communication and risking—risking that they might think I am stupid or weird. I think I ran a lot of people off by not telling them how I felt. They got the impression that their presence in my life didn't really mean anything. I presented myself as being real cold and independent and self-sufficient. I had always perceived the need for help or support as a weakness. If I was emotional with people or was vulnerable and let people know exactly what I felt about them, I was weak. I have more people in my life right now as a result of just saying little things like 'I really like being with you,' or 'I'm really glad we have become friends.' "

Debbie is a marketing consultant, organizing meetings with physicians. Professionally, her attitude has shifted since she did the training. "It's not the actual job skills that have changed. I had those. But I have shifted out of some negative attitudes. The training has helped me to look at each moment as a new possibility to really create some magic. I have more freshness in my meetings and that has shown up in results.

"The other thing is that I really stepped up to the pump and I said 'I want more responsibility' rather than sitting back and thinking that somebody was supposed to come to me with it. I picked up the phone, called my manager, and requested that we sit down and talk about my career goals and about what I would like to do within this organization. I've become more in tune with what I need in order to be effective in the job.

"I also began to recognize the importance of personal relationships. Again, for me, it's just being vulnerable, showing the softer side, letting people know I really care. Knowing that it's okay, that it doesn't make me a fool to let someone know I care about them—even if they don't have the same feelings for me. I have to be true to myself and I have to be honest in my communication with others, which I had not been. And that means with my family as well. When I finally did, the rewards were there.

"One time I picked up the phone and called my Dad. My daddy is a person who does not express his feelings or emotions. I called him and he asked if I wanted to talk with my mama. I said 'No, I called to talk to you.' I told my Dad that it's real important that he tells me he loves me. He did and has again since, which is a real shift for us. Being that open and honest with him was really risky for me. It began a whole different relationship for us.

"I'm more relaxed. I still thrive on intensity, but I've relaxed a lot. I'm just not so set in my ways anymore. There wasn't much room for error before, and I really used to beat myself up if I thought I made a mistake. Now I just acknowledge my mistakes and I move on. I think it comes from being more at ease with myself and liking myself more, being less critical of who I am. Not being so hard on myself has created the opportunity for others to be open and relaxed with me.

"Before the trainings, I was so black and white on everything. You know, this is the way it is, and that's it. Period. I would never say 'Okay, so let's take a look at some other possibilities here.' I was just not open at all to any other way of seeing things. Instead of holding things as 'This is the truth with a capital T,' the training showed me that there are other ways of looking at things."

The Physical Universe Is The Ultimate Guru

20

We all have times when we fear that someone is going to uncover the "truth" about us and blow our racket—reveal that our public image is just a con, and that there is nothing underneath it. The source of this self-doubt is a discrepancy between who we claim we are and what we actually think and do. We expend a lot of energy convincing the world that our image is authentic while covering up what really is authentic. Then, we wonder why people don't seem to appreciate certain qualities of which we are particularly proud. Sometimes our self-images and our public images don't match, our public and private "conversations" are different. To cite some examples: you may say that your word is gold, but in fact, not keep your word some of the time; or, you may say you live as a stand for responsibility, but there are instances in which you believe that circumstances beyond your control have determined your experience; or, though you say you are authentic and care about people, there may be times when you are uncaring and insincere, not letting others see and hear what is really important to you; or, you may have everyone convinced that you are the quintessential results-producer, but you hide the fact that half of the time you sit home watching TV.

In this chapter, I am asking you to distinguish between what you say you are committed to and what the *facts* say you are committed to. In other words, where, if anywhere, is your understanding of yourself inconsistent with what an objective outsider would observe? This could be a very confrontive process. It takes courage to even acknowledge that there are times when your actions don't line up with who you think you are (and who you think you have everyone else convinced you are). To evaluate yourself strictly in terms of your results, to calculate your effectiveness in terms of straight facts, reveals truths people often prefer to ignore. It will be necessary to your breakthrough that you look candidly at your results and consider what they reflect about the sincerity of your commitments and your effectiveness at fulfilling them.

THE PHYSICAL UNIVERSE IS THE ULTIMATE GURU

Why focus on results? Doesn't that remove much of the humanity from life? I am not recommending tunnel vision about results, nor that the drive to achieve specific goals become your prime motivator. There is definitely more to life than just that which can be measured by your results. However, a healthy relationship with your personal statistics will assist you to create a climate for breakthrough. Your results provide the most reliable form of feedback about both your commitment and the effectiveness of your practices. They will spell out what is actually happening and what is missing. As the title of this chapter says, the physical universe is the ultimate guru. You can count on the facts of the physical universe to indicate how it truly is. The facts don't care what you think about them, whether you like them or hate them, or anything else about your interpretations of them. Having a relationship with the physical universe in which you honor the information offered to you through facts and statistics can empower you to take effective action.

Take a moment to explore your relationship with statistics. By statistics, I am referring to the measurable results in your life. Include all areas—physical health and fitness, education, career performance, money and material wealth, community involvement, leisure, marriage, children, home, and so on. Write your answers in your journal.

- Do you set goals? What are the goals you are currently working toward? Are your goals specific and measurable, or broad and general?
- Do you regularly take stock of your results, evaluating your progress on and completion of your goals? When was the last time you reviewed your goals and your progress on them?
- Do you avoid setting goals or recognizing your results?
- Are you able to reduce things in your life to specific results? Can you look at situations and simply say, without justifications, either 'I did it' or 'I didn't do it,' 'it happened' or 'it didn't happen'? Or, do you generally tell a whole story about why you did what you did or didn't do what you didn't do?
- Take some time to reflect on your results—distill your results down to the straight facts.

YOU ARE WHAT YOU DO

Imagine there is a scoreboard that keeps an objective record of your actions. It doesn't hear what you think, what you feel, what you want; it isn't convinced or impressed by your image, it doesn't take into account how hard you try. It doesn't deal with 'why not,' it only sees 'what is.' It only tracks what you do. If you say you will be somewhere at noon and you are there by 12:05, the score doesn't show that you were *only* five minutes late, it just scores one in the category called "You didn't do what you said you were going to do." If you promise yourself that you will work out four times this week, and you work out three times, the record doesn't say "Well, gee, at least you did better than last week." It scores another one in the old "Didn't do" column. Imagine if people were to hold you to account for the exact record on that scoreboard—if no one cared how badly you *wanted* to do what you said, or how sincerely you *intended* to follow through on it. Imagine how it would be if you were only defined by what you actually *do,* and if you only interacted with people on that basis. It may sound harsh, but actually, at an important level, you do get defined by what you do.

Think about it. We are social beings, and people can only perceive you by what you say and do—no one has any idea what goes on in your private conversation about yourself. As far as anyone else is concerned, you are what you do—no more, no less. People will listen when you have an explanation for why you didn't do something you had promised, or when you have a great story about how you accomplished something you set out to, but your interaction is ultimately based on what you did—the result and its consequences.

What you think or experience in your secret world has no bearing except insofar as it assists you to function better in the world. I say this not to malign psychological or spiritual experiences or other inquiries that don't yield immediate, tangible results. But if an inquiry doesn't have some relevance in the physical world, then you would be better off alone on a mountaintop meditating for the rest of your life. In theory, there may be more to human beings than meets the eye. In practice, however, what else do you have to work with? Counting on "potential" is folly. If there is something else, it has decided to remain concealed, and therefore cannot be directly addressed or effectively probed. God or higher powers or spiritual laws hold their own place in the human experience. Your journey in those domains need not be excluded from your development in the domain of transformation and breakthrough that Lifespring addresses and vice versa. To gain power over your presence in the physical world, though, you must first recognize that, as a human being, you can only intervene and make a difference through your actions in the tangible human world.

The discrepancy between your opinion about yourself and what the facts say about you, between who you think you are and who your actions say you are, skews your perception of reality. Our culture disdains much of what is authentic about being human. You are subtly encouraged to blend illusion and reality when it comes to your identity. That undifferentiated union of fact and fancy suggests, then, that there is some real "you," some essence that is separate from what everyone else sees through your actions. This pretense covers up that you only exist, and can only be understood by virtue of your actual participation in the world, your practices and actions, the activities in which you engage. In other words, "What you see is what you get."

DOES ANYTHING MAKE A DIFFERENCE BESIDES WHAT YOU DO?

If you are what you do, of what significance are your thoughts, feelings, opinions, desires, fears, and so on? They are part of your experience, but they do not ultimately determine who you are or the difference you make. Who you are and the difference you make is based on what you do.

Try this: Wait for a clear night. Go outside—if possible, to the mountains or by the ocean. Look up at the stars and tell them what you think, feel, hope, wish, and fear. Really get excited about it. Be convincing. Show the stars the full extent of your longing, sadness, happiness, insistence, anger, fear, confusion, helplessness. Shout, cry, whimper, plead, threaten, laugh, flatter, whisper, pout. How do the stars respond? What kind of difference does all that information make to them? What is caused in the universe as a result? All this is to say, much of what "feels" or "seems" very important to you doesn't make any real difference in the world—the universe doesn't care about any of it.

A commitment to operating primarily in the domain of thoughts, feelings, and desires, fosters evaluations like "That makes me feel good (or bad)," "I think that is wrong (or right)," "I wish I had $1000 to spend on new clothes." We constantly have such thoughts, feelings, and desires, and they are nothing to ignore or avoid. *But,* those conversations, which we typically focus on in the drift, will not produce action, resolve breakdowns, or open possibilities. Rather, they will tend to make you right about your beliefs, solidify the status quo and diminish the possibilities for anything new to occur. Functioning in the domain of "You are what you do," on the other hand, is a way to counterbalance the impotence of the drift. Living by the motto "You are what you do" engenders such questions as "What's missing and what is the source of the solution?" "What's my next move?" "What will it take to have a wardrobe that works for me?" Such a framework will tend to evoke ideas, feedback, promises, and requests that will move you forward in a productive direction. No "inner" process will make anything real happen in your life unless it is part of a process that affects how you are in the "outer" world.

WHAT YOU DO VS. WHAT YOU THINK YOU DO

Do you ever experience people not responding to you the way you think they should, or misunderstanding you altogether? Or wonder why people don't seem to recognize how much you care about them? Or why a friend got offended when you had no intention of insulting him? Or why people don't seem to appreciate your sense of humor? Or why your expertise isn't sought out? Maybe you harbor the illusion that those traits are obvious (you know how caring, considerate, hilarious, and capable you are), but are not actually taking the actions in your life which reflect caring, consideration, humor, and competence to others.

Our interpretation of ourselves is so transparent to us that we assume it's what others see too. We get confused. We believe that what we *think* is real *is* what is real. We assume that how we see ourselves is an accurate reflection of how we appear to others. We think that we are who we *think* we are, not what we *do*.

Ask yourself the following questions and look at how consistent your actions are with your concept of yourself. Enter your thoughts in your journal.

- List your ten best attributes—qualities you are most proud of and that make you a person worth knowing.
- Go back over your list one item at a time. List the things you've done recently that demonstrate each one.
- Are you able to substantiate every claim?
- Are you actually 'showing up' in the world the way you think you are? Would an objective observer describe you the same way you have described yourself?

Where do you look to see how you show up in the world and how effective you are? Your own experience of yourself is unreliable; it is colored by your interpretations, your ego, your need to look good. The evaluations of others may be worthwhile, but that depends on their levels of honesty and competence. There is information available to you, however, that is a reliable source of feedback: your results— what you actually *do*. The facts, minus your assessments and justifications, illuminate where you are telling the truth about yourself and where you are buying an illusion; where you are effective and where you are not. You can only make corrections if you are accurate in interpreting the facts.

You might have noticed a contradiction in the last couple of sentences above. How can your interpretation of the facts be objective—minus assessments and justifications—when it is just that, interpretation? On a purely abstract level, everything in the human condition is interpretation. To be human is to interpret. The challenge to you is to school yourself in streamlining your interpretations down to the most basic reports. Train yourself to hear the difference between statements like: "I can't meet with you today," and "I would meet with you today, but I don't think I can"; "I missed the appointment," and "I don't see why she got so mad—I was only a little bit late"; "I wish I had two more weeks to complete this assignment," and "I have three days to complete this assignment"; "I didn't get the account," and "If only he had understood what I was trying to explain to him, I'm sure I would have closed the deal." Your psychological assessments and editorial additions to the plain facts can conceal the chief problem or issue, obscuring the truth and prohibiting effective action. While you can't *not* interpret reality, you can master the distinction between self-serving stories and impartial observations. It is in that distinction—in being able to observe the facts impartially—that you will find the tools for becoming more effective.

WISHING, HOPING, WANTING, TRYING

Acting on what you wish were true rather than on what is really true will only frustrate you. Say you are a man, five feet, eight inches tall, or a woman five feet even, and you think that life would be better if you were taller; people would find you more attractive, you would be more noticeable, and you would command more attention and respect —generally, you would pose a more powerful presence. All these are matters of interpretation. What would our objective "You are what you do" scoreboard say? The scoreboard would say "This is how tall you are." The world doesn't care whether you like your height, whether you think the tax structure is fair, or whether you would like to earn more money. Remember how impressed the stars were by your thoughts, feelings, and desires. The car dealer isn't going to sell you a new Mercedes because you wish you had enough money to buy it or because you think you deserve it. Wanting something does not cause any action to take place. Any results that occur while you are wishing, hoping, or wanting will only be lucky accidents.

The bedfellow of wishing, hoping, and wanting is trying. Take another example. You make the claim that you are committed to getting in shape. What it will take is to modify your eating habits and begin working out regularly. You set a goal for yourself of losing ten pounds in the next month and exercising three times a week. So you decide to cut down on desserts, and you buy the hottest new aerobics video. And you actually do cut down on desserts and you actually do work out. You feel better about yourself, which is nice. But, you look up one month later and you have not lost any weight. You really did cut down on sugars and fats. And you ate a lot of those healthful whole grains. A lot. You absolutely did work out regularly, though. Well, okay, one week you only worked out twice. But you had to stay late at work three nights that week to finish the big project. Regardless of how hard you *try*, saying you are committed to something, and becoming the practices which will effectively make it reality are different.

Our culture would like to ignore that distinction. We spend too much time and energy analyzing, acknowledging, and increasing our awareness of what isn't working, and not enough time changing our practices accordingly. We hate to admit when something that we are doing, especially something that worked for us or someone else in the past, isn't working now. We get stuck on the "try track." We think that because we tried, we accomplished something. We give ourselves a lot of credit, and expect others to acknowledge us for how hard we tried.

If your practices lean to wishing, hoping, wanting, and trying, an ability to interpret the facts won't accomplish anything. Analyzing how you got to where you are, predicting where you will end up, gesturing at taking action, or taking the wrong action, is a lot easier and less threatening than changing yourself and your behavior now in a way that will effectively intervene in the future.

THE OBSESSIVE

What about the other extreme? What about the person who is obsessed with results? The person driven to be number one, to constantly be topping his or her own and everyone else's performance? If you are that person, you are constantly checking your results. You don't have any trouble recognizing what is working and what isn't. In fact, you live to have the statistics validate your claims and are adept at correcting what doesn't comply. The statistics don't assist you, they run you. You, in a sense, have become your results. Record in your journal:

- What is your experience of life? Are you generating satisfaction?
- Do you hold people and things primarily as means to an end?
- Is the achievement of specific goals sometimes a hollow victory? Does it generate meaningful fulfillment?
- Is your life so much about 'destinations' that it is acceptable to you to be relatively unfulfilled during the 'journey'?
- When you are ninety years old, looking back on your life, will you merely have an impressive checklist of results, or will you also have an experience of having lived a meaningful life?
- What is missing for you?

Always maintain a healthy relationship with statistics, but if and when you are driven by obsession, broaden your criteria for accomplishment to include qualitative fulfillment as well as quantitative results. Instead of asking yourself the question "How many, by when?" ask "How many, of what kind, by when, and why?"

BREAKDOWN

Being committed to telling the truth about the facts will also empower you during the inevitable breakdowns and setbacks that you will encounter. Being effective is not about eliminating breakdowns, but about performing responsibly in the face of breakdowns. If your relationship with your results is unsound, you will tend to view breakdowns and mistakes as personal failures. Not failure like "Oh, I didn't do what I said I was going to do," but failure like "I must be some kind of incompetent, ineffective, uncommitted jerk." You become your failures. Eventually you stop looking at your results (your only reliable source of feedback) because it is too painful to face the possibility of failure.

On the other hand, not turning failures into personal invalidations liberates you to take a stand about correction and resolution. You don't become your failures, but rather you *have* breakdowns. Being in constant recognition without taking every setback personally allows you to correct breakdowns effectively. A breakdown isn't a direct reflection of you, it's something you deal with. And, come on, who doesn't get into situations where things don't turn out? In fact, the more you are operating on the edge of peak performance, the more likely you are to experience breakdowns. I'm reminded of a friend who liked to wipe out on the ski slopes. She said that if she weren't falling periodically, she knew she wasn't pushing her limits.

YOUR RELATIONSHIP WITH RESULTS

So how about some practical tips about developing a so-called "healthy" relationship with statistics? First, ratify from your own experience that the physical universe is the ultimate guru. Train yourself to make the distinction between facts and your prejudiced assessment of the facts. Next, identify an area of your life in which the universe proves you are effective. Where, based on the results you produce, are you doing well? Allow yourself, then, to look just as frankly at another area in which the facts are not so favorable. Notice your assessments and justifications in each case. Boil each case down to the black-and-white facts and ask yourself the questions: What have I accomplished?, What haven't I accomplished?, What's missing?, and What's next? Do this in areas in which you excel as well as in areas in which you are experiencing breakdown—it is just as valuable in both cases. Second, build a network of people who are honest and competent to give you feedback. In other words, a group of folks who are committed to your commitments. These may be friends, coaches, outside experts, family members, but must be people you will listen to seriously. "Use" this network, check in with these people regularly. There is no need to defend yourself, just listen and learn.

Finally, don't believe a word I have said. Stop, think, and look at how it is for you in your life. Live in the questions. Are you what you do, no more, no less? What implications does this have for you? What possibilities are there for you? What are you going to do about them? There are opportunities for transformation in struggling with these questions, and no opportunities in dismissing them without consideration.

Remember that after all this talk about statistics and "actual" results, all that makes a difference in your life is the stand you take about them. Your ability to discern the facts as objectively and impersonally as possible will assist you in taking effective action only if your commitment is to effective action. It isn't your results that make you a person worth knowing; it is your approach to life, of which your results are merely a by-product.

21

Charlie Morf

GRADUATE PROFILE

For Charlie Morf, forty-nine, the president and CEO of a billing services company that operates throughout California and Oregon, the Lifespring trainings were all about people. "One of the great beauties of the training is that so many people came into my life who are so valuable to me.

"Part of the magic is that in the training environment I had a chance in the exercises to be so open and honest. I said things and got things off my chest in an arena that was so caring. I really had an experience of trusting people. The rewards have been remarkable.

"Since the training, it has become a habit.

Now, I regularly have conversations of the same caliber I experienced in the training; open, honest, trusting, caring.

"Because the training is experiential, it never, ever goes away. I have never had a day without something from the training having an impact. For instance, during the training, I expressed things that I had always hidden from people—thoughts or feelings that I thought made me less than I wanted people to think of me. Now, every time I act the way I used to, it hits me right in the face. I now have new choices about how I am. When I start pulling my old tricks, I see it and I know that I can either change it, stop it, or hang in there, knowing that it doesn't work. The risk of acting differently than I always did isn't any worse than letting the knowledge that I'm being dishonest eat my heart away. Once you've done the training, you know how safe it really is to be honest, and you are acutely aware of the distinction between honesty and dishonesty.

"Sometimes I make conscious, deliberate choices about behaving differently, but often the changes in my behavior are unconscious. In my marriage, my natural reaction to conflict has always been to get defensive. Now, though, when something happens that two or three years ago would have caused me to get my defenses up, I look up twenty minutes later and notice with amazement that I didn't have the habitual thought and take the habitual actions I always automatically used to in similar incidents. I do some things differently now, it works out much better, and my ego survives.

"The training was one of the turning points in my life. Not like I needed to change or was in desperation somehow. In other words, I didn't go into it wanting my life to be dramatically different, and it really hasn't changed much on the surface. Yet my perceptions of what I hold as valuable, especially people, are entirely different. That change has totally transformed the quality of my relationships.

"It has made a tremendous difference in how I am with people. For one thing, I am more at ease with myself. People are open with me in conversation because I am open with them. I give myself permission to say things that I formerly would have held back from people. We all have ideas about what we should and shouldn't say to people we are in relationships with, whether it's family, business, friendship, or just a casual acquaintance. We say one thing out loud, but think something else. It's so obvious to people when you are not being straight with them. It's also obvious when you are absolutely telling somebody how you feel and you're really honest and straightforward. Whether it's criticism or compliment, it's obvious that it's coming from your commitment to that person. The inner worth of every person is so evident to me now; I search for that and speak to that rather than looking only at my judgments of them. I don't accept anything but people's magnificence.

"I gained a whole new concept of how people can contribute to me and how I can contribute to them. It has become habit to listen more to people, even people whom I never would have associated with before the training. When I first went to the Basic, I wouldn't talk to three-quarters of the people in there. I had my judgments of everybody. There's the teenybopper. There's the little cutesie. There's the unhappy old lady. I just sat there in judgment of every single person. Lo and behold, guess what I found out? They were all in judgment of me too. It was remarkable to interact with each other, when normally we wouldn't have had anything to do with each other. Many of those people are now an important part of my life—two years later—as friends and supporters.

"Not only do people contribute to me when I listen to them, but I contribute to them by listening. So often when people come to me, they're not looking for anything except someone who'll listen to them. I always thought there was more to it, that I had to perform a more active role than just listening in order to help someone out. I found out that men in particular are so used to giving advice, especially when talking with women, that it really gets in the way of just listening. Two years ago, a woman could have been telling me about an experience she'd had and inevitably I'd chime in with how I'd handle the situation. She wasn't asking for my worldly advice, she just wanted to tell someone the story. Ninety percent of the time, people aren't interested in advice, they just want to get something off their chest, clear up their own thoughts, share. I find I'm talking *at* people less, and listening more. I've learned how to just be a good bouncing board.

"I take a lot more risks with people than I've ever taken before. The small risks seem to have as much or more of an impact than the sensational risks. Sometimes it blows people away when I simply come back after having had a conversation with them and say 'I haven't said something I meant to say.' I'll be on the phone with one of my managers, and we'll fall into the pattern of business talk. We'll be talking about a project that we're working on and I can tell he or she is sandbagging me, but I let it go. I don't want to criticize them. And I hang up knowing that we haven't accomplished anything other than the fact that we both know that we hedged the issue. We haven't said what we really wanted to say. I'll pick up the phone again and say 'You know what, we just had a conversation that wasn't really a conversation. Let's start again.' It's amazing how people react. They usually are grateful and tell me that they were thinking the same thing.

"Risking with my wife is more difficult. There is so much at stake with the person I'm in love with. And really, she's the person it's most important for me to be absolutely honest with. My wife and I were separated for a year. When she left, I had no idea what was going on, in my stupidity. I'm very proud of the fact that we're back together. I know I would never have been able to do that had I not taken the Basic Training. I believe we have been able to come back together and be in the relationship in a way that works for both of us because we finally got really honest. It has made us both much more loving to each other and to everybody else.

"I had never thought about my needs in a relationship. And I never thought of saying to a woman: 'Here are my needs, honey.' My history taught me that the man is the provider and protector, and that's how I have been with every woman I've ever been in a relationship with. Make sure the lady is taken care of, but don't try to change her life. I would back off of what I needed in the relationship. Then when it didn't go well, I could be very self-righteous, saying 'I did all of this for you and you didn't do anything.' I found a lot of reasons why I am that way. I also recognized that it doesn't work and that I am responsible for it not working, so I have the opportunity to change it.

"What happened between me and my children after the training was one of the most precious things that has ever happened to me. Particularly with my son, because I think we had more tension between us. When I got divorced from my first wife, their mother, it was very difficult for me not to be with my kids. I felt very selfish about the choices I had made. When Robert, my son, came to live with me and my current wife, there was a lot of friction between him and me. Since going through the trainings, we have never been closer. We're not holding onto a lot of judgments about each other. We have our problems, but there is unconditional love, support, and honesty."

Charlie's son, Robert, comments that "I had a lot of resentment that after the divorce with my mom, he just wasn't there a lot of the time. I held a lot of grudges from that. I held it all in. I hated that my father was away. I was at the age where a boy really needs his dad. I was playing baseball, I needed help with my schoolwork, and he just wasn't there. After going through the Lifespring trainings, having been through those same experiences, our communication level is great. We talk about everything."

Charlie says, "The training taught me the golden rule. Do unto others as you would have them do unto you. It's so simple, but seems difficult to put into effect. It takes real effort and it takes time. The training made me a more caring person. Now I'm not just willing, but eager to demonstrate my caring for people. It has made me more effective with people. My relationships are much deeper.

"I experienced time in a whole new way during the training. Back then, the trainings went quite late into the night. I was surprised that I didn't get tired. I never got tired. I completely shifted my experience of time. I now find I have so much more time than I ever had before. I'm on the board of directors of Big Brothers. Big Sisters of Marin, as well as on the board of directors of a home for abused children. Before the trainings I thought I was too busy to do anything like that. I never had as much time for people as I do now.

"One really profound experience I had in the training concerned the death of my two-month-old daughter in 1969. I thought I had finished mourning her, but actually I had bottled up my mourning for years. This may sound trite, but I started thinking about how fragile life is. Someone said in a training 'Life is not a dress rehearsal.' It's so true. This is it, the real thing. How I play it is my responsibility.

"I had a breakthrough about responsibility in the training. Acting like I'm 100 percent responsible makes me a little more concerned about people; it inspires me to function at my best. It isn't based on evidence. I may not actually be causal, or to blame, but it was a breakthrough for me to consider that I am responsible for everything. No blame, no credit, just responsible.

"Taking the opportunity Lifespring offers changed my outlook completely. It gave me something that I didn't even realize was missing. I was crying for it, but didn't know what it was or where to get it. There is no question in my mind that we owe it to ourselves to take responsibility for our personal transformation."

Authenticity

22

Being authentic, being actually and precisely what you claim to be (and claiming to be precisely what you are), requires that your behavior prove your claim. We said earlier that you are what you do. If what you do is aligned with your claims about your identity, then you are being authentic. However, if you claim to have a certain set of commitments, while your actions serve other ends, you are being inauthentic. Your commitment to some goal is only authentic when that commitment shows up in your actions; when that goal, rather than all others, actually governs your behavior.

INAUTHENTICITY

Before defining authenticity, it is useful to distinguish between different types of inauthenticity. Authenticity and inauthenticity are not absolute categories, but are different ways of being and acting; you could be authentic in one respect and inauthentic in another. You're inauthentic when your behavior is aimed at convincing yourself and others that you have certain commitments, not because you really do, but because seeming to gets you certain payoffs. Your real commitment is to the payoffs, not to that to which you claim to be committed. Inauthenticity can take at least three different forms which I'll call: (1) drifting, (2) bad faith, and (3) dogmatism.

DRIFTING

The drifter is a person who just does what anyone else in his cultural circumstance would do in life. He is a conformist, doing what is expected of him, what is normal. Whether the drifter is inauthentic or not depends partly on why and how he is conforming to the cultural drift. It's possible to seem to be conforming while leading a rich, satisfying life. What makes the drifter inauthentic is that his main goal is to remain comfortable by avoiding the anxiety that arises from being abnormal or having to cope with abnormal situations. A drifter will spend his life either trying to avoid situations that might result in his looking "abnormal," or, when confronted with such situations, will try to force things back to what is "normal" and comfortable. Being normal is the highest priority of the drifter, more important even than the well-being of the people involved or the positive outcome of events. For example, there are various "normal" ways to be a father in our culture, but these norms don't anticipate having a homosexual son. A drifting father will not be able to respond creatively to this situation. If he can't talk or coerce his son out of his homosexuality, he will do whatever he can to deny, repress, or avoid it, to the point of denouncing the relationship altogether. While he claims to have a genuine commitment to his son, his ultimate commitment is to looking like a "normal" father. He does not take his own stand about fatherhood over and above the conventional cultural stand. In situations like this, when cultural norms conflict with each other, you must decide who you are in the matter.

There is an especially shallow and sterile way of conforming with the drift that is prevalent in modern society due to the character and pervasiveness of the mass media. When you conform to the media drift, your interpretations and behavior are mediated by the norms celebrated in the media. These norms are intended to sustain and expand the influence of the mass media itself, and they will tend to flatten and blur peoples' ability to make distinctions.

In all cultures we learn through our involvements in concrete relations, like our family, church, and school. In a media culture, those relationships are shaped, in large measure, by the media. "Looking good" in a media culture like ours is all about conforming to the prepackaged images created by the media. Our identities and interpersonal relationships take on a highly generic character. Insofar as you strive to emulate these generic types, you open yourself only to the commitments and concerns that are represented in the mass media and are available to the generic drifter.

Consider the areas of your life in which your inauthenticity may be characterized as "drifting." Use your journal to write your thoughts.

- How important is 'looking good' to you?
- Where did you get your definition, formula, or model, for looking good?
- Have you acted inauthentically merely to avoid looking bad, even when you were aware that some other creative action would have been more effective? What were the circumstances? What were the consequences?
- Where in your life are you 'drifting'? What action would you have to take to stop drifting? What will it entail? Will you take that action? When?

BAD FAITH

The "bad faith" brand of inauthenticity is much more cunning than the drifting brand. This person is the great pretender. In bad faith, you develop a certain inauthentic identity, not with the intention of conforming, but of reaping specific payoffs traditionally associated with that identity.

To illustrate, consider the difference between two ways of being a "suffering mother," one of which is authentic and the other bad faith.

An authentic woman might genuinely suffer for the sake of her children in the sense that she has to work hard and forego other opportunities for their benefit. But what governs her behavior is her concern for her children and it just so happens that, in her circumstances, suffering is an unavoidable consequence of that. If she could serve her children without suffering, she would.

On the other hand, the mother who suffers in bad faith is less concerned with the children than with the privileges that suffering mothers earn. Mothers whose circumstances are such that they have to make sacrifices for their children get attention and acknowledgment. Moreover, a suffering mother has a legitimate excuse for not engaging in activities which, if not for her commitment to her children, she would otherwise have to pursue, given the principles she claims to value. Therefore, insofar as a woman convinces herself and others that she is a suffering mother, she can provide excuses for herself and lay moral claim on others. The mother who suffers in bad faith is willing to suffer in the name of her children even when suffering isn't necessary to promote their welfare and even when it runs contrary to their welfare.

Acting in bad faith is a way of attaining the goodies that go along with a certain identity, without actually being committed to the principles of that identity. It allows you to say "I deserve X because of who I am, or because of my circumstances" even in situations when you would otherwise have to take effective action in order to get X. In this way, it can relieve you of your own responsibility to act; you automatically inherit benefits that you would otherwise have to earn.

Of course, bad faith has a heavy price as well. You artificially narrow your opportunities by cutting yourself off from any possibilities that don't reinforce your chosen identity. If you are going to be a suffering mother and enjoy its entitlements, you have to play the part. Also, it is manipulative; to the extent that you use suffering motherhood to coerce attention and deference from others, you are engaged in a kind of fraud. In spite of the fact that you must pretend not to know what you are really up to, this fraud and manipulation will inevitably color your world, and will affect how you experience yourself and others. Since it is mandatory that you not be exposed, you will often see others as threats. You'll have to be constantly on guard, suspicious of peoples' questions and opinions, worried that they might expose you. You also experience yourself as cut off from others, as not "really" the person they think you are, and as not really deserving the attention and sympathy they tender.

It's a tough one to admit, but examine the possibility that you are acting in bad faith somewhere in your life.

- Where are you reaping benefits that you have not actually earned? What are the benefits?
- How is that inauthenticity limiting you?
- What would you have to give up if you became authentic in that area?
- What would you gain by being authentic?

DOGMATISM

Dogmatism is a more subtle form of inauthenticity than either drifting or bad faith. You don't hold a dogmatic commitment because it is normal (even if it is), but because it is "right." Unlike the drifter, you may take a stand that can actually bring you into conflict with the norms, and unlike the person acting in bad faith, who exploits cultural norms for their moral entitlements, you will hold the norms in contempt if they contradict your sense of what is right.

What makes a commitment dogmatic is the very strong, righteous way you hold it to be objectively and absolutely valid. You believe that this commitment automatically supersedes any other considerations in all contexts. Your cause is objectively the most important cause to which a person can be committed and allegiance to it supersedes all other allegiances in any situation. There is little room for new possibility in dogmatism.

The payoff of dogmatism lies in avoiding the ambiguity and the anxiety of having to choose one course of action over another when faced with the twists and turns of life. You are relieved of the burdens of interpretation and choice and of the risk of really participating in a vulnerable way. Dogmatism is a way of not taking responsibility for your actions because you claim not to be acting out of interpretations, but out of absolute principles.

The cost of dogmatism is loss of freedom. Its rigidity and inflexibility cuts you off from other points of view and from the richness that accompanies the ambiguity of human life.

Ask yourself these questions about dogmatic inauthenticity:

- Is there any example in your life in which you hold a dogmatic interpretation of right?

- Do you believe in objective standards of right and wrong, worthy and unworthy, good and evil?
- What prices do you pay for your dogmatism?
- What are the payoffs you get?

AUTHENTICITY

Unfortunately, we are much less clear about the nature of authenticity than we are about inauthenticity. One way to characterize authenticity is to contrast it with its converse.

In being authentic, your chief concern is neither to be normal and safe nor to be abnormal in a way that justifies special treatment, nor to put yourself on the side of right. In fact, your commitments sometimes require behavior that runs contrary to the norms and will not produce the payoffs associated with drifting, bad faith, or a dogmatic commitment.

In being authentic, you will simply do what you do. In contrast to drifting, however, in situations that cannot be anticipated by the cultural norms, which demand a creative response, you will be more flexible than the drifter because you are willing to take a stand that puts you in opposition to the drift. If necessary, you'll give up looking good in favor of the unique demands of your particular ideals and goals. So, the authentic father who discovers he has a homosexual son can deal with the situation creatively although it is not provided for in the norms of his culture. He doesn't flee from the situation by denying it or repressing it. Of course, in responding to his son, the authentic father will have to draw upon cultural resources and these will limit his room to maneuver. But how he draws on these resources will depend on how they contribute to the welfare of his son rather than on how they reinforce his own identity as a certain kind of father. Authenticity requires that you think for yourself, struggle with questions rather than simply go along with the drift. An authentic stand exists within the drift, but is not aimed at fitting in with the drift.

Neither is the authentic stand like the stand taken in bad faith or dogmatism. That is, as an authentic individual, you are not committed to generating special moral entitlements or being on the side of right. Authenticity is governed by concern for the welfare of the individuals involved and for the conditions of each unique situation. Thus, the authentic mother lives out of her commitment to her children. She may suffer when it is necessary to benefit her children, but doesn't suffer for the sake of its payoffs. In fact, she is willing to forego being a suffering mother even in situations where the cultural norm might be to suffer. Authenticity is *not* unconsciousness, manipulation, or avoidance—which characterize drifting, bad faith, and dogmatism, respectively.

You cannot necessarily identify authenticity by someone's results. An honest shopkeeper may be motivated by profit rather than by a commitment to the truth, having discovered that his reputation for honesty has attracted many customers to his shop. The result, that he tells the truth, is the same under normal circumstances. One test of authenticity would be to see what he would do when the external circumstances were varied. If, for instance, it became highly profitable to make some dishonest claims about a product he sells, or if he were underbilled by a vendor. Of course, in life we are constantly confronted with complexities and subtle variations forcing us to grapple with the authenticity of our own commitments.

Use your journal to begin an inquiry about authenticity by considering the following questions.

- Have you ever taken a stand about something even though it puts you in opposition to cultural norms?
- How would you define authenticity?
- How do you know when you are being authentic?
- How do you know when you are being inauthentic?
- How do you undermine your authenticity?
- When you are inauthentic, what is more important to you than being authentic?

SYMBOLS: HAVE-DO-BE AND DO-HAVE-BE

Being authentic does not automatically render results, and results do not necessarily indicate authenticity. If your behavior is motivated by a sincere commitment to certain concerns, then the probability of achieving the results that fulfill those concerns is high. However, there is no guarantee. You can control your motivation and your competence, but you cannot always control the results of your actions. The results you have are symbolic of, but not measurements of, your authenticity.

In our culture, we worship symbols. We look to our results for fulfillment and to validate our claims about who we are. For instance, we believe that money equals power, freedom, choices, security, respect, happiness. Consumer industries capitalize on the link between symbols and satisfaction. A car isn't a car, it's a feeling; a pair of jeans doesn't clothe you, it makes you sexy. Billions of consumer dollars are spent every year on such promises. You are not just buying products, you are buying the subjective, qualitative experience that those particular products promise you. People look to the things that they *have* and the things that they *do* to provide them a desired experience.

But are those things really the source of your experience? Take the example mentioned above of a car. All American sixteen-year-olds long for their own cars. Why? Because the cars give them freedom, responsibility, power, status, independence. And while you're at it, why not go for the ultimate dream car? After all, a Rolls Royce or a Ferrari will make you feel classier, richer, sexier, more powerful, and more prestigious than a Buick. When you actually get your dream car (or dream job, dream marriage, dream home, or whatever), it may not turn out to give you the experiences that you had counted on. You may fulfill those desires temporarily, but the car itself is merely the object of that experience, not the source of it. In fact, not only is a car not the source of freedom, power, and prestige, but sometimes your car can appear to cause the opposite experience, like when it breaks down in the middle of nowhere in the middle of the night, or when you have to take time off work to take it into the shop, or when you drive away from the dealership after having written them a $750 check for standard maintenance, or when you really don't feel like washing it. And, to look at it another way, can't you have the experiences of freedom, power, and prestige without the car? In place of our commitment, we substitute the symbols that we think generate the experience we are looking for.

The false link between symbols and experiences does not stop at material acquisitions. For example, many people believe that when they get married, they will suddenly have security, stability, friendship, companionship, family, sex, unconditional love, excitement, nurturing, and so forth. Anyone who is married can tell you that, in fact, much of the time they feel *less* secure, nurtured, loved, and everything else, than before they married. Furthermore, do you need to be married to be happy, secure, and nurtured? Marriage is merely an arena for you to express yourself. Your relationship with your husband or wife isn't an acquisition that comes with a lifetime guarantee of satisfaction; it is a platform on which you can act out, explore, and transform the conversations you have about marriage, commitment, family, and other matters.

The "Have-Do-Be" structure of interpretation leads you to believe that symbols will inherently provide you with an ultimate experience of fulfillment. But another variation of the paradigm, "Do-Have-Be," says that it is the process of acquiring the symbols that causes us your experience. If you work harder, making X number of calls every day, you will have more sales, will earn more money, and will, therefore, be successful, rich, happy, and respected. You are still looking to an external agent or activity to determine the quality of your life.

Of course, to go to the other extreme and say that what you do and have doesn't matter at all smacks of the old "go meditate on the top of a mountain for the rest of your life" philosophy. What you do and have definitely matters. Your behavior is your trademark, and your results, while not foolproof reflections, are checkpoints or representations of how effective your actions are. The error our culture teaches us to make is to look at activities and material objects to fulfill us.

We develop this very early. Look at babies. A baby catches on quickly that crying gets attention from Mom and Dad. All they have to do is let out one or two good "wahs" and they are immediately center stage. The love was there already, the "wah" was just a mechanism for controlling it. The baby, however, thinks that the "wah" caused the love. Similarly, symbols and activities do not determine quality of life, but we often believe they do.

I promise that your life is full of "Have-Do-Be" and "Do-Have-Be" thinking. Examine it for yourself using your journal.

- Think of examples in your relationships that demonstrate the 'Wah = Love' theorem. In other words, strategies you use to get attention or that others use to get attention from you.
- Ultimately, do you produce results for the sake of producing results or for the sake of something else? If something else, what?
- What experiences do you believe will be yours as soon as you have Car Charming? Relationship Charming? Body Charming? Children Charming? Job Charming?
- Is it possible to have those experiences without having the symbols?

"AS SOON AS"

As inclined as we are to look to external circumstances to derive meaning and fulfillment from life, it's easy to be gripped by the "as soon as" delusion. Life will really take off as soon as you get married, get your degree, make your first million, get a new car, get promoted, buy a house, move into a different neighborhood, have children, get rid of your children, turn forty, get divorced. As soon as, as soon as, as soon as. This is doomed. According to this strategy, there is always another "as soon as." Not only can you never do enough or have enough, but your higher goals and aspirations get lost in the drive to conquer your next symbol. Meanwhile, you are only minimally engaged in your present circumstances, always with your eye on the future. Life is about ready to begin to commence to get started, just as soon as. . . .

Life is not a dress rehearsal. While you are putting off what is most important to you until just "as soon as" you reach the next benchmark, life is racing by you. While you are busy preparing yourself for the day you finally grasp that carrot dangling on the stick in front of you, your possibilities for "being" remain untapped. Your future is predictable, and it's the kind of future that leaves you with the question, "Is this all there is?"

AUTHENTICITY: BE-DO-HAVE

The "Be-Do-Have" model says your commitment is the source of your experience. Your commitment is authentic if you are engaged in behavior that encompasses your higher ideals and aspirations. "Be" is not a tool with which you can regulate the universe—you cannot ultimately control what happens to or around you in your lifetime. Integrating your principles and your actions gives you wholeness, worthiness, and fulfillment.

The concept "Be" is also not a mechanism for guaranteeing what you "Have." "Be" is the stand you are. If you are genuinely committed to world peace, and work for world peace with sincere dedication, it is not guaranteed that you will achieve world peace. If you are committed to making a million dollars this year, and strive industriously toward that goal, it is not guaranteed that you will make it. You can control your motivation and your effectiveness, but you cannot control the external world. The "Be" part of the picture is about the powerful possibilities for achievement and excellence opened by the integrity of the human being. Regardless of the outcome, you will fortify your integrity by authentically pursuing your ideals.

"Be-Do-Have" sounds like a formula. Unfortunately, there is no recipe for authenticity. "Be-Do-Have" is a reminder of the human mystery mainly because the concept called "Be" is so vague and perplexing. "Do," meaning engaging in actions with certain goals, is fairly straightforward, as is "Have," the results of your actions. But what is "Being?" While the inquiry into ontology, the nature of being, has had the most powerful influence in my life personally and in the work we do at Lifespring, it is beyond the scope of this book. "Be" is that dimension of a human being that determines what and who you are, what you stand for, what you are up to on the planet. From your "being" emerges your character, concerns, and actions.

In the jargon phrase "Be-Do-Have," "Be" refers to your commitment to your higher ideals and aspirations, the goals toward which your behavior is directed. "Be-Do-Have" asks you to pick and formulate your life projects such that what you value profoundly is authentically expressed with passion, precision, grace, and power.

Drucie French-Cumbie

23

GRADUATE PROFILE

"Before Lifespring, I thought I was an ordinary person. Now I know that we are all extraordinary people. The distinction lies in the context in which I live. I create that context."

Drucie did the Lifespring Basic Training in 1982, a month after her husband did it. "In many ways, our lives were quite successful: We come from strong, supportive families; we both hold graduate degrees; we had made significant progress financially and professionally.

"When we married in 1978, I left my job as a producer/director of medical videotapes and channeled all my energies toward 'our life together.' My husband had just started a new business that was thriving but demanding. I did everything I could to support him in his work—I entertained; I renovated a townhouse in Georgetown; I got a job as a consultant when we needed extra income; I handled family matters. I made all my choices based on my obligations—my duties as a wife, daughter, daughter-in-law, and so on.

"The trap I was in was that, at the end of every day, I found myself insufficient. No matter how hard I worked, I had never done all that I should have. I was not happy and was beginning to entertain the nasty suspicion that it was my husband's fault. That was my frame of mind when I heard about Lifespring.

"I had done some experiential learning in graduate school, so the concept was not new to me. And neither were the basic concepts covered in the training. I'd been exposed to them before. But the effectiveness of the Basic was incredible.

"My circumstances haven't 'changed.' I'm a wife and mother. I just finished building a new house. My husband's business is still expanding—it takes most of his time and a lot of mine. Yet, everything is different. I make my choices based upon my purpose in life. I'm living an extraordinary life in perfectly ordinary circumstances.

"Before the training, I had been defining my life by traditional, social roles. The only possibilities open to me were those which were already established. I measured my value by how perfectly I lived up to those standards. My insistence on perfection destroyed the possibility of joy. Joy was the very thing that I was yearning for. I felt that all my dreams were disappearing into a grim swirl of duty and obligations.

"One of the biggest breakthroughs I had in the trainings was about urgency, the sense that now is all I have and it is important that I take action now. I had been living my life more passively than I live it now. I noticed in the trainings that I am not so much afraid of dying as I am afraid of not having done my life's work. I began to discover my purpose in living. It wasn't hard to identify. I simply looked to the obvious. I want to make a positive difference in this world by teaching people to live more lightly—more enlivened, less burdened, more gracefully. The Lifespring trainings are not religious, but as I continue on this path, I am experiencing a reawakening of my spirituality. I have a sense of divine grace that guides me. That is what I mean by living *gracefully*. I'm learning to listen.

"I don't worry anymore about what I should be doing. Opportunities show up on my plate. Where before I would stew over whether or not I should take on a project and how I would do it, now I know immediately whether or not a particular opportunity is part of my life's work and I commit to it without the debate. I don't just limit myself to those things I already know how to do anymore. There is not much room for breakthrough in limiting myself that way. Am I ever afraid? Sure, always. But if a goal is in alignment with my purpose, it is worth the risk. ·

"I've learned to simply jump in when offered an opportunity to stretch my limits. Since doing the training, I've announced that I would raise money for the March of Dimes, Special Olympics, Peace Child, Youth at Risk, a project directed toward resolving the conflict in Belfast, the Center for Conflict Analysis and Resolution, and several others. I was on the board of trustees for the Lifespring Foundation for two years. Every time I take on one of these commitments, I don't have the vaguest idea where the money is going to come from. Every time I make this kind of declaration, a little voice reminds me that I might fail. Sometimes the outcome surpasses my expectations. Sometimes my results are what I consider mediocre. Each time I have learned something and contributed something to the world.

"When I choose, commit, declare, the possibilities for action flood in. People show up to assist me. Resources become available. Fear is replaced by creativity, discovery, challenge. Through the training I have had a great sense of freedom because I approach life differently.

"I've come a long way since the Basic. I no longer see my life as a grim downward spiral of obligation. I'm still changing diapers, cleaning up after the dog, giving cocktail parties. I still have days when I feel overwhelmed by cars, houses, family, pets, clothes, dirt—days when I experience life as burdensome. I still lose my temper with my daughter and my husband. All the responsibilities that defined me and, I thought, confined me, are still real. I just look at those things differently. They are not burdens for me anymore, they are resources. They are gifts, like a trust fund, that can be squandered or enriched. I know that when I experience life as burdensome, what is off is me. From that point of view I have the power to re-choose. It is like that button that I've seen people wear: PBPGINFWMY—'Please be patient. God is not finished with me yet.'—and neither am I."

In all of her work, Drucie has been unfolding her potential as a woman. "Having a woman trainer in one of the trainings, I began to re-examine what it is for a woman to be powerful in this world. The power of her femininity impressed me. I looked at my beliefs about women and how women are a very important, healing part of the balance in life. Yet, I noticed that if fulfilling that meant conflict, I would usually back off. I'd look for ways to make a difference in people's lives that didn't end in confrontation. There was a big shift for me there in being willing to face conflict on the way to fulfilling a bigger purpose. I know that if I'm in a loving relationship, it works to act out of that commitment and not passively wait for the relationship to evolve. Sometimes that involves conflict.

"Since moving to Washington, I found myself becoming more and more the kind of person who lived behind the gates in the wealthy neighborhoods. I didn't know any old people, and I didn't know any kids. I only knew people who went to college and were just like us. I had evolved in the archetypal yuppie mold. I chose it, but I was unconscious that I was choosing it. I had been kind of a funky teenager, but somewhere along the line between sororities and private schools and degrees, I left a whole big part of me behind. It was great for me to be dealing with people in the trainings that I didn't usually have any contact with. That was also part of the reason I did the trainings because I was looking for a way out of the limitations of my life-style. I really liked being outrageous and being a part of the whole world, not just an ever-refining, narrowing segment of society. Being in the trainings allowed me to assist and be assisted by different people. I was served up these wonderful opportunities for knowing people and doing things that I would never have done. Jumping into those opportunities was a big part of my commitment to broadening myself.

"Another whole story is how Lifespring affected how we are as parents—the joy we take in it. To begin with, how it was for me when I was delivering the baby was dramatically different because of having done the training. I was in control in the sense that I felt accountable for what was going on, but also totally trusting of what people were telling me to do and how to do it. I know that my husband and I would have never worked as such a great team if we hadn't done the trainings. It was wonderful. It was miraculous for us and if I hadn't gotten anything else out of the training, the difference it made in how I handled the birth of my daughter was fantastic.

"Lifespring was and continues to be an opening for us as a couple. When our marriage gets stormy, tumultuous, and difficult, the trainings have provided us a context to work it out. When there is something as important as having a child that we want to do together, we're now able to get our egos out of the way, which is something we never had done before.

"I don't really think I would have had my child and this house and a sense of my life's work if I hadn't done the training. I may still have discovered my purpose, but I don't think I'd be as committed or as effective at pursuing that purpose. The trainings are causal, they set something off in my life. My life has been greatly enhanced by what I discovered in the training room."

Relationships/ Empowering Others

24

Millions of words have been written over the years, particularly in recent years, about how to make relationships work. You know as well as anyone the litany of generic ingredients for a lasting, fulfilling relationship: open communication, partnership, fun, common or similar goals, commitment, and so on. You also know as well as anyone the frustrating and painful chasm between knowing what works in relationships and doing it. I assert that what it takes to make the leap from being informed to being effective in relationships lies in asking a different and more basic question than "How?" Rather than studying how to make relationships work, explore what relationship is.

Before reading on, what is your definition of a *relationship?* Write your definition in your journal.

WHAT IS A RELATIONSHIP?

To relate is to interact or to act upon one another. The big mistake we make is that we think a relationship has a life of its own, that it is something we can have or be in. A relationship is nothing. No thing. Synonyms for the word relationship include connection, affiliation, alliance, association, interconnection, interdependence, correlation. None of those words speak of a concrete entity. The language of relationship is dynamic. Relationships are continually unfolding events. You aren't "in a relationship," you simply relate to other people.

It's interesting that so many people say they want to *have* a relationship. There is no "a relationship" to have. Isn't it also interesting that you'll rate your relationship with someone as great (or a mess) at any given time, as though there is something there other than your actions and your interpretations and the actions and interpretations of others.

Explore your interpretations:

- What are your criteria for a 'great' relationship?
- What are your criteria for a 'bad' relationship?
- Where do you look to find the evidence to prove whether a relationship is good or bad?

Being in relationship is the state of being human. In our culture, we learn that we exist as individuals, thereby concealing our social nature and fostering a mood of aloneness. Relationships are thought of as things that occur periodically against a background of individual separateness. This is merely a learned interpretation. Remember, human beings are fundamentally social beings, not separate units. The individual "I" doesn't exist except as it correlates with the rest of the world. "I" is the name we have given to a complex set of relationships that occur in the vicinity of our physical bodies. It is our natural state as human beings, even definitive of being human, to be in relationship.

To say you don't have enough relationships or you aren't in a relationship is absurd. The project at hand isn't to *have* relationships as though there is a way to get them, to be *in* relationships as though they can be entered and exited, or to *make* them work as though they are pieces of machinery. Relationships are not things. Rather, the project is to cultivate a way of being related that is extraordinarily fulfilling.

A relationship is merely an opportunity to relate with another person. Like any opportunity, what you do with it is up to you. Your commitment determines what and how each relationship in your life is. There's the tricky use of language again in the preceding sentence, implying that a relationship is some "thing" that can have a quality all its own. All there is for you to do is play with people, participate with people, be in conversation with people, love people. What comes out of those interactions isn't "a relationship." Those interactions *are* the relationship. What comes out of those interactions is the next opportunity to interact.

Consider the following questions as part of your own inquiry into relating:

- How does this inquiry into being related alter your perception of relationships?
- How does the definition of relationship you gave in the previous section limit what is possible in your relationships?
- Are you trying to figure out a way to turn this inquiry into a formula for a new way to interact with people so that your relationships work better or so that you have more of them? If so, notice that you are still holding relationships as 'things.'
- What does having your relationships 'work better' mean?
- If there were a theme to describe how you tend to interact with people, what would it be?

A WORKING RELATIONSHIP TAKES WORK

Relating effectively demands a lot of you. It requires rigorous thoughtfulness, disciplined behavior, genuine concern for others, and relentless courage. Passively drifting through relationships is like a salesman sitting in his office waiting for the phone to ring. It may ring a few times, but there isn't a sense of aliveness or personal accomplishment, and no reliable basis for future growth. Likewise, when you are out in the world "waiting for the phone to ring," only responding to people when they come to you, and then responding inauthentically or otherwise thoughtlessly, you'll remain safe, but you can count on a low level of aliveness, accomplishment, and possibility. We are thrown to *not* demonstrate our caring for others, to *not* be thoughtful, and to *not* risk in our relationships. Hence, it will take deliberate effort and supreme determination on your part to shift your behavior in the face of our culture's norms.

Being thoughtful of others includes being disciplined in your practices and being willing to make choices based on your concern for the well-being of others. This means that you sometimes will find yourself making a choice that is less pleasurable to you than if you were only considering yourself. Please go find where it is written that a relationship is supposed to be an endless source of pleasure. Who said that a rewarding relationship equals constant bliss? Who promised that being committed to having your relationships work means you will always be having fun? The potential for satisfaction multiplies when you view a relationship as a vehicle by which you may contribute to another person, and together contribute to the world, as opposed to your approaching that relationship as an end in itself, or as something that is primarily concerned with *getting* pleasure. Love is a commitment that supersedes and sometimes requires you to set aside the desire for immediate gratification in anticipation of a higher purpose.

Here are some questions for your reflection:

- Do you operate on the belief that 'good' relationships should just happen, and should not require work?
- What thoughts and feelings do you have when a relationship does require you to work?
- Think of a recent example of a time when you set your own needs or desires aside to accommodate the needs or desires of someone else. What feelings did that evoke in you? For example, on the one hand you may have felt predominantly resentful, guilty, regretful, manipulated, unsupported, neglected, martyred, and so on. On the other hand, you may have felt predominantly supportive, loving, appreciative, giving, valued, and so on. How do you honestly feel about the give-and-take aspect of your relationships when it demands something from you?

CONCERN FOR OTHERS

Relating, defined as acting upon another human being, implies an outward focus. Yet most people do not act out of a commitment to having their actions serve others. Of the people who do act out of the commitment to serve others, many do so at the expense of their own nurturance. Serving others does not mean selfless sacrifice, but really considering what impact your actions have on other people and acting in such a way as to give yourself and others the greatest possibility to benefit.

Remember the Golden Rule? Do unto others as you would have them do unto you. If you lived according to that rule, it would be a priority for you that other people's lives worked. How you are with the receptionist at the office, and the grocery clerk, and the plumber, and your children's teachers, and your neighbors, would proceed from your commitment to treating them with the same dignity and care that you would like to receive. What does that really boil down to but *thinking* before you act, and acting out of concern for others? Most people don't harbor malicious intentions. But most people forget to honor, for example, the receptionist as much as they honor their family and dearest friends. Most of us are in too much of a hurry. It takes a willingness to take action a bit above and beyond the call of duty to demonstrate the kind of respect and compassion for other human beings that is empowering.

Think about it.

• How do you fit into the scheme of things? You have an effect on people and on history whether you like it or not. In your day-to-day interactions, are you responsible or irresponsible about the impact your actions have?

EMPOWERING OTHERS

Whom do you hang around? They are probably people who empower you in one way or another. Sometimes empowerment means being contributed to and other times empowerment means making a contribution. Empowerment is the key to rewarding, enlivening, loving relationships.

An act of empowerment intervenes in a relationship in three ways. First, it provides something that was missing. Everyone involved is now complete in a way in which before they were incomplete. What was missing and what can be given depend upon the unique blend of the people involved. With your spouse, empowerment may mean a demonstration of love. With your coach, it may mean being challenged, being confronted about what isn't working or praised about what is working. With your colleagues at work, it may mean honest feedback about each others' ideas or performance. Second, empowerment causes a shift in practices so that the people involved are left more competent and renewed in their commitment. Third, empowerment leaves you with the question: "What's next?" It enables you to look up from the grind and explore where you are headed and what possibilities lie before you.

Under no circumstances does empowerment *have to* feel good or make you happy. It can and often does, but doesn't have to. Gaining or providing a missing distinction and changing one's practices are not always comfortable experiences. Empowerment isn't about feelings, it's about being enabled to become more nearly who you can possibly be.

Having your relationships work means relating with people in a way that is mutually empowering. When you stand for empowerment, the actions and behaviors that make relationships fulfilling will emerge. Rewarding interactions and relationships will be the rule, and breakdowns the exception, not the reverse. Of course, you alone are responsible for being empowered. Blaming someone else for not empowering you is a sell out. You can stand for being empowered in the face of *any* circumstances.

A necessary part of empowerment is being clear on your commitments, being able to speak your commitments, and being able to listen to the commitments of other people. Others can only get behind you in what you are genuinely committed to, and you can only empower them in what they are committed to. When you are listening for people's commitment and speaking your own, others discover new possibilities for themselves out of interacting with you.

What it takes to be both empowered and empowering, what is called for, is a reorientation of yourself. There is no reason or evidence for it, it doesn't make sense, it isn't logical. There is no "how to." Following instructions for empowerment is totally insufficient. It can only be freely given because it is what is called for. You must create this one yourself, be responsible yourself, take a stand yourself. You must come to terms, very deeply and very personally, with what you have said you stand for.

LISTENING

When you listen to others, what do you hear? As we have made clear earlier, to be human is to interpret. What you hear when you listen to others isn't necessarily what they are saying. What you hear is your own interpreted version of what they are saying. There is no way to avoid interpreting, but there is a way to have listening be empowering. Unfortunately, in the drift of average interaction, we are uncommitted speakers and listeners, thus disempowering our conversations with one another. Rehabilitating your capacity to listen is crucial to transforming the quality of your relationships.

Listening and speaking are symbiotic practices. They are either mutually effective or mutually ineffective. Unfortunately, the drift of our culture is toward ineffective speaking and listening. It is a vicious circle. When you know that whomever you are talking to probably isn't listening very closely, you aren't as careful about what you say. And vice versa—when they know that you aren't really committed to what you are saying, they only listen half-heartedly. Do you ever notice that when someone demonstrates that they really have been listening rigorously by asking you for clarification or by questioning you in some other way, it can throw you off—that you suddenly get confused or uncertain about what you were saying or lack the confidence to face questions? Most conversation is thus reduced to idle talk, stories, gossip.

When you communicate at the level of stories, narrative, and opinion, there can be no empowerment and no breakthrough. Breakthrough comes out of your vision and your commitment to live by your word. This means saying what you mean, meaning what you say, and listening to what people say, not what you think they mean. Only when you cut out your stories, reasons, and justifications can you discern what appropriate action to take. And only when you do not support the stories, reasons, and justifications of others is there the possibility of empowering them.

How can you be a committed listener or speaker? You can begin by starting an inquiry into your own speaking and listening habits. Below are some questions to assist you.

- When you listen to others, where is your focus? Are you focused on yourself or on what they are saying? In other words, are you thinking about whether you agree or disagree with them, whether you like what they are saying or not, what you will say next, or are you simply trying to understand what they are saying?

- If you were to critique your own listening, what changes would you recommend to yourself?
- When you speak, how do you react if someone questions you or disagrees with you? How important is being right to you? How does your need to be right impede your speaking and listening?
- If you were to critique your own speaking, what changes would you recommend to yourself?
- How often do you interrupt people before they finish their thought? How often do you finish people's sentences for them?
- If you are an interrupter or a sentence finisher, try this for the next twenty-four hours: Stop it. Don't interrupt people and don't finish their sentences for them. Let them talk until they are finished, and only talk once they stop talking. Notice how often what they end up saying is *not* what you were thinking it would be. Notice how the conversations go places they couldn't have gone if you had interrupted.

RIGHT / WRONG VS. POINT OF VIEW

We often have hidden agendas when we are in conversation with people—to sell them something, convince them of something, validate our own beliefs, and so forth. I say that the only empowering agenda to have is the desire to contribute to another human being. An essential element of serving other people is to acknowledge them and their points of view. Human beings are thrown to being right. In conversation, when your focus is on yourself, which is usually the case unless you train yourself otherwise, you are all about gathering evidence to prove that your opinions are right or that differing opinions are wrong. Little gets accomplished in such a conversation. If everyone agrees, you end up with a "Mutual Admiration Society," but little possibility for breakthrough. If everyone disagrees, you do your best to convert each other, or dismiss each other altogether.

Playing the right/wrong game is both frustrating and exhausting. It is futile. It cripples your ability to think. Given that human beings are pure interpretation, who said yours are any more right than anyone else's? We all think that our opinions are facts, and that any differing opinions are stupid. As long as our priority is to be right, we don't have to think, to evaluate our own opinions, to change. One of the most empowering, supportive, inspiring things you can do in a relationship is freely acknowledge the other person's point of view. The acknowledgment contributes to them, and the opportunity and willingness to see the world a different way contributes to you.

Here are some more questions and suggestions on speaking and listening:

- What happens to your speaking and listening in the face of disagreement?
- Notice your human tendency to 'come from' being right. How do you react when someone else is making you wrong?
- What ways do you subtly or overtly make yourself right and others wrong in relationships?
- Are you someone who is always making yourself wrong? If so, what are you really being right about?
- What would it take from you to genuinely recognize the validity of points of view other than your own? (You can *say* you acknowledge a different point of view and still *mean* 'I'm right!')

FEEDBACK

You are who you are by virtue of the meta-conversation you share with the world. Furthermore, other people only exist in your conversation about them. How you are perceived in your interactions with others determines the possibilities for those relationships. Being open to hearing about how you show up in the world according to others greatly enhances your chances of being effective in your relationships. The direct feedback of others, while it can be painful or uncomfortable (which both criticism *and* acknowledgment can be), can be incredibly empowering if you stand for it being empowering.

Feedback is available every time you turn around. It takes many different forms: verbal communication, body language and facial expressions, staring, offhand comments, smiling, touching, eye contact, avoiding eye contact, laughter, applause, crying, promotions, raises, grades, questions, and so on. The physical universe is also a source of feedback. Your results and the facts reveal valuable information about you.

How do you deal with receiving the feedback that is available to you? Do you listen to it, ignore it, invalidate it, space out, use it to be right about your beliefs or to make others wrong?

How do you deal with giving feedback? Do you sugarcoat it? Do you invalidate it before or after you give it? Are you indirect about it, or mean about it? Do you withhold it altogether?

Think of someone whom you find unattractive. The criteria do not have to be physical. Answer the following questions about this person:

- What characteristics do you find unattractive about that person? List them.
- What characteristics do you find attractive about that person? List them.
- What about that person do you perceive as similar to you?
- How do you perceive yourself as different than that person?
- Now, think of someone whom you find attractive. Again, the attraction does not have to be physical. Answer the same questions about that person.

Giving or receiving feedback is only verbalizing what is *already there anyway*. Whatever assessment is expressed in the feedback was already present between you and that other person. Speaking it merely makes the private conversation public. Our judgments about whether feedback is positive or negative are only our judgments. Most people find that sharing conversations that include feedback, even when it is not what they would consider "positive" feedback, result in greater intimacy and new possibilities for the relationship. One caution about feedback: It can be damaging if not expressed in a caring way. Your responsibility is to deliver and receive feedback in a context of caring.

With respect to reading the feedback of the universe, look around at your relationships. Your relationships are a perfect representation of how you are showing up to people. The abundance in your relationships and your satisfaction or dissatisfaction with your relationships is a reflection of your stand about relationships. If your relationships don't work, you are a stand for relationships not working. If your relationships are empowering and fulfilling, you are a stand for that. If you are willing to take one hundred percent responsibility for the quantity and quality of your relationships, the feedback of the universe and of the people who care about you will make you a more competent player in the relating game.

Continue your examination of the value of feedback with the following questions:

- Who are the people in your life who, if asked, would probably have helpful feedback for you about how it is to be in relationship with you?
- Have you ever asked for their feedback? If not, why haven't you?
- Will you ask? If yes, by when?
- Who are the people in your life who, if you had their permission to give them feedback, you could contribute to by doing so?
- Why haven't you?
- Will you? If yes, by when?

ACKNOWLEDGMENT

We all too often sweep under the rug one of the most empowering forms of feedback: acknowledgment. When you are acknowledged by someone, do you invalidate it, change the subject, or deflect the praise away from yourself? Do you make a point of acknowledging others, or do you let their contributions to you go by unnoticed?

You can make an immediate difference in your relationships if you do the following:

- Make a list of people you need to acknowledge. The acknowledgment could be for a specific thing they did, or for their general contribution to your life. Communicate those acknowledgements in the next twenty-four hours.
- When you are acknowledged for *anything* in the next month, listen to it carefully and then make only one response: 'Thank you.'

INTIMACY AND COURAGE

It's no wonder that intimacy is such an issue for people, given how challenging it is simply to give and receive acknowledgment and honest feedback. Everything you think of when you think "intimate"—closeness and sharing of a personal and private nature—is at the same time desirable and intimidating. Can you figure out why intimacy and courage are in the same section?

It takes tremendous courage—which is defined as the mental or moral strength to venture, persevere, and withstand danger, fear, or difficulty—to meet the conditions of an intimate relationship. Vulnerability is perceived as dangerous given the conversation our culture has about relating to one another. Guess what? If you interpret other people as dangerous, you will have plenty of opportunity to gather evidence to prove that they are. Or you can stand for a different interpretation, one that allows for mistakes, hurt, and forgiveness. Then, the only evidence you'll be able to gather is that people—including yourself—are human. Within the freedom to be human lies the possibility of intimacy.

Begin to explore what intimacy means to you by reflecting on the following questions or requests.

- Define intimacy in your own words.
- Do you hold a grudge for a long time, or 'get off it' quickly and move on?
- How do you express anger? Do you withhold your anger? Do you blow up? Do you express it covertly through resentment or some other emotion and concomitant behavior? Do you face the person toward whom it's directed? Do you tell the story to all your friends, but never confront the person who is the source of it?
- How often do you censor things you think of but are afraid to say? What are you afraid of that keeps you from saying what's on your mind?
- Are you comfortable revealing feelings or thoughts that you consider of a personal nature?
- Are you comfortable when others reveal to you feelings or thoughts of a personal nature?

THE THREE PILLARS OF RELATIONSHIP

The quality and durability of any relationship rests on three pillars. I'll describe these pillars in terms of a "primary" relationship, but the same pillars are applicable to any type of relationship. The pillars are sequential; the first must be solid in order to be a foundation for the second, and both of the first two, in turn, must be healthy for the third.

The first pillar is a responsible, authentic, committed self. You must have some clear idea of what you stand for in life. Your commitments in life will shape how you relate to others. A key to the first pillar is recognizing that you are responsible for how your relationships show up for you. That you are one hundred percent responsible isn't "the truth," it is a stand that you can take that will give you the freedom to participate authentically and passionately in your relationships.

The second pillar is a connection between two people that is appreciative, caring, and honest. One distinction between primary relationships and other relationships: Let's face it, to have a primary relationship that works, you have to like the person, have an affinity for that person, want to spend time in that person's presence. For other relationships to work, such affection isn't necessary; the principles of respect, contribution, and concern for others enable you to open the possibility of an empowering, effective, productive relationship with anyone.

The third pillar is a shared purpose—something that can be accomplished better by two people together than by one alone. For a lasting relationship, it is not enough that you be solid as an individual, and that the connection between you and another be deep and caring. How long can you gaze romantically into each other's eyes? You must turn outward together toward a contribution to the world that you can make better together than separately. For many married couples, their shared purpose is their children, but it doesn't have to be.

YOUR RELATIONSHIPS

The following is an exercise for a general inquiry into your relationships:

- Describe your relationship history. What are the main themes, issues, and patterns in your relationship life? Take ten or fifteen minutes to write this down.
- Look back over your description. What percentage of your description concentrated on facts, and what percentage on feelings? What percentage on negative experiences and what percentage on positive experiences? What percentage on past relationships and what percentage on current relationships? What percentage on what you got from the relationships and what percentage on what you gave?
- Now, retell your relationship history. Only this time—whatever you emphasized before—focus on the opposite. For example, if you emphasized the negative before, emphasize the positive this time around; if you focused on your feelings last time, focus on the facts this time; if

you focused on past relationships before, focus on current ones this time.

- What are the prices people pay for being in relationship with you?
- What are the rewards they receive?

Rosalie Maretsky

25

GRADUATE PROFILE

Rosalie Maretsky is a Mary Kay senior sales director in Los Angeles, California. Her professional explosion is an example of astounding transformation. She has gone from working for free in a friend's office, because she didn't believe that anyone anywhere would be willing to pay her, to earning over $70,000 a year running the Mary Kay sales unit that she built from nothing. Reflecting on her Basic Training, Rosalie remarks, "I look back on what takes place in those five days, and the transformation the training causes is mind-boggling! I guess confronting myself has always been my best teacher. When I had the environment to really look at myself in a way that I had never looked before, and to see the gifts that other people have to offer, it deeply affected me."

Rosalie took the Basic in 1980. "My life since the training has been incredible. I look at all that I've accomplished and am stunned by what I'm doing now. If anyone had told me eight years ago that I'd be doing this eight years later, making this kind of money, having this much fun, I'd never have believed them.

"If you had seen me ten years ago, you probably wouldn't have thought I was very different from now. I had a very good facade, but underneath I had very little self-confidence, and my self-esteem wasn't any better. I played it very safe. I would not risk at all. I had my moments when I did fund-raising events, being the president of this volunteer organization, or vice president of that one. But, when the event was over, I went back into my little world and stayed there. I was terrified of risking."

Rosalie has been married to her husband Sandy for thirty-six years. They have three children and two grandchildren. Rosalie and Sandy did the Basic Training together. "My son, Alan, was the one that originally got myself and my husband into it. He told us in December of 1979 that he was doing this training. I was very upset about it. I really felt that he didn't need it. I was wondering where I had failed and why he would want to take this course. I knew that this was a crazy thing he was getting into. Then, after he did it, I started to notice his life changing. I always considered him a workaholic, I didn't see him having fun in his life. He wasn't dating. All of a sudden, he changed his job and started working what seemed like regular hours. I saw him going to parties and starting to have fun.

"When he asked my husband and me to go to a Lifespring Guest Event, I said: 'No way: I'm not going because I'm very put together; I'm very aware; I have all the answers; I know what it's all about and I don't need it.' Sandy and I had done Marriage Encounter in 1976, so we already had closeness and good communication in our relationship.

"Finally I agreed to go to a Guest Event with Sandy, but there was no way we would sign up to do the training. I really had a preconceived idea about it. I told Sandy that if they're wearing robes or anyone looks dirty or like a bunch of hippies running around, I'm leaving. I really thought it would be like that. When I walked into the Sheraton Universal, it was mobbed. I walked in and saw people hugging and was completely turned off. We stayed and sat through the whole event, but I didn't hear a thing that was said. It went right in one ear and out the other.

"During the night, we bumped into a friend of ours, a woman I really looked up to. I thought she was fabulous. She told me she had done the Basic Training and it was great. I remember thinking that if she would be enthusiastic about this, there must be something to it. So I started to soften up a bit and considered doing it. Sandy and I eventually just talked ourselves into it, agreed to do it, and enrolled. I didn't really know why I had decided to do it or what was drawing me to the training other than the encouragement of this woman. I didn't think about changing my life, my relationships, my career, or any of that.

"When I went into the training, I was very resistant. I wasn't open at all. I only went because I had committed to my son to do it. I sat there that first night wondering why I was there. I said I was definitely *not* going to participate here. I'd just keep my mouth shut and sit there and observe. And that's what I did for the first two days. I thought the Ground Rules the first night were silly. I had no patience with the people and their questions.

"When I finally got engaged in the training, it was Friday during the day, while I was doing the homework. The training was on the week of my forty-sixth birthday and I was feeling very depressed, which is unusual for me on my birthday. I got very sick with a bad cold. By Wednesday before the training, it was a full blown case of bronchitis. I remember Sandy said to me that if I was sick, maybe we shouldn't go. I ended up doing my martyr mother routine, saying that we owed it to our son to do this. So I was sick on Wednesday and Thursday nights. Thursday night there was a lecture about illness and health. My ears really perked up. There I was in the training, sick; I had always had colds all my life, I grew up with illness around me— my mother had died of cancer, my father was epileptic. I really started listening and looking at the role that illness had played in my life— how I had relied on it as an excuse, how I had dealt with it with my parents. Then we took the homework that was on accountability to fill out before the Friday night session. I was so sick the next day I left work and just went home to bed. I lay in bed all day by myself. And all I had was time to think. That was where I really got the training. The homework got me thinking about what I was getting out of having this cold. Then I remembered that big sign hanging over the stage in the training that said 'What Are You Pretending Not to

Know?' The more I lay there, the more I thought about it. By that afternoon, I couldn't wait to get back to the training to share about everything that was going on with me.

"I was the second one picked to share that night. When I got that microphone in my hand, I was shaking like a leaf. I started sharing about this illness. I had a tremendous fear of dying. I had seen my father passing away, then my mother. The trainer said something to me that was so important. I don't even remember exactly what he said. It was simple, but in that moment it had a huge impact. When I sat down, I felt like another person. First, spending that whole day of thinking about accountability, and then sharing with the group, was very dramatic for me. Once I had really jumped in Friday night, that was it for me. I was in the training full force.

"It was interesting doing the training with my husband because, of course, his experiences were totally different from mine. We did it together basically because I wouldn't do it without him. I wouldn't do anything without him. At that time, I really thought that I needed him there to pick me up in case I fell down. I really thought like that. Then, when I started to get so excited about the training, I was upset that he wasn't acting the way I was. Of course, he was going through it at his own pace."

After the Basic Training, Rosalie began stepping out in her life, particularly in the area of her career. "For so many years I put myself down. I had really lost so much of my self-confidence. I was married very young, at seventeen. Then, I had my first baby at eighteen. So my whole life in the fifties was raising kids, being the typical home-maker. In the fifties, I thought a woman's place was in the home; you cooked and cleaned, took care of your husband and children, partici-pated in the PTA, and all that.

"Here's an idea of how low my self-esteem was before the train-ings. When my youngest, my daughter, was thirteen, my mother passed away. It was a very traumatic illness, and it was very hard on me. My daughter was thirteen, so I didn't have to stay home with the kids anymore. I needed to do something. I was so terrified about going out to find a job. I would look at the want ads every day and close the paper. Nobody would want me. I didn't have any qualifications. There was nothing I could sell. I called my girlfriend who was man-aging an office and asked if she needed any help. I told her I would do whatever she wanted, I just wanted to get into that office. I told her she didn't even have to pay me. She had just fired someone and needed help on the phones. I helped her out every day without pay. And I was excited about it. That's how much I valued myself. That's what I thought I was worth. After a while, it turned into a paid position, for something ridiculous like $600 a month. That was a beginning for me."

Rosalie has spent over twenty-five years doing charity work and it was after she took the trainings that she began to take on more responsibility. "I was and still am very involved with City of Hope. I was asked to be the chairman of their annual luncheon. That was huge. At that time, about 1300 people came to the luncheons. For the first time, they wanted to put on a two-day affair, and they wanted me to take it on. At first I shied away from it, I didn't want the responsibility. I didn't want to deal with the women involved, to cope with all the different personalities. The magnitude of it was overwhelming. Finally, I accepted and I did the luncheon. I know I only accepted because, after having done the trainings, I knew that there was so much I could do." Remember, this is the woman who years earlier had worked for free because she didn't think she could do anything worthwhile. "Years ago, there's no way I'd have been able to work with all those different people in a position of leadership. I'd have let them walk all over me. I'd have been a nervous wreck and I would have hated the whole thing. Once I took it on, I saw that I really can work with people. All the problems I used to have were insignificant. I had really learned in the trainings how to work with people, and how to communicate in a way that creates results. The luncheon was a huge success. We raised more money than we ever had."

A couple of years after doing the trainings, Rosalie first heard about Mary Kay Cosmetics. She was first attracted by a brochure she read that "spoke the same tongue I know so well. They talked about risking, about expanding your comfort zone, about responsibility, teamwork, and giving. I was looking for something that would support me in living by my principles, and here was this company that applied those same principles, a company that would support me in taking what I had learned in the trainings and putting it into action in the world. I saw this as a great vehicle to touch a lot of people and make a difference in their lives.

"I started out slowly, playing it safe again. I was just going to have fun. Then I decided if I was going to invest money in this, I was going to learn everything about this business and be the best I could be. That's how it started five years ago."

The key to Rosalie's success is her competence in empowering the women in her unit. "I gained all my expertise in working with people through the training. I can work with a woman who comes in shy and insecure, and teach her how to work with people. When she starts to blossom, I step back and let her rise. There's a lot of rejection out there and a lot that these women have to face, but in the process, they start to learn that they really can make things happen. That's where I make a difference in people's lives. I motivate them and teach them everything I know to be great, not mediocre. I don't believe in anything small. I believe in going all the way to the top, and that means being the best you can be. Empowering people, to me, is the most exciting thing that anybody can do.

"I really do feel that I owe my success to Lifespring because I don't think I would have ever gone into business for myself given my insecurities and low self-confidence. I wouldn't have taken the kinds of risks I have taken. I have set and hit goals that were totally out of the realm of possibility. According to the numbers, we never should have done it. I don't look much at the numbers. I look at the people and see what I can do with people. The results have been phenomenal. I've had this sense of mastery about shooting for what seemed impossible, and we have done it, year after year.

"Empowering others is a full-time job. I love doing it. If I look back at where my life was before the trainings, I didn't have any idea about empowering people. I was more into running around and shopping, working with charities, and those kinds of things. It just wasn't very fulfilling. I have had to give some things up in the process. For one thing, my friendships have changed. I'm still close with my friends, but I won't just sit on the phone and gab for two hours in a day anymore. I would like to give myself more time with my friends, but I would never trade my life for where it was before. If I have to give something up in the process, then I'm willing to pay the price.

"I've learned to lighten up and enjoy what I'm doing, even when I stumble. When I get too serious, I'm not creative, and I don't produce results. When I stay light, have fun, the results come. That's what the training is about for me. It's not a magic wand you wave over yourself and suddenly your whole life is different. It's about applying what works in your life."

What's Next?

TAKING ACTION

Franz Kafka said that "A book must be an ice axe, to break the sea frozen within us. If the book in our hands does not wake us, as with a fist that hammers on the skull, then it isn't worth reading." The thing with this book is that it is just one long request for you to take action in your life. The information presented here and the inquiry opened in these pages are only context-free theories, stories, and open-ended questions—unusable without your commitment to applying them. They are dead unless you breathe life into them in the context of your own life. The impact the book has for you, like anything, is really up to you—and the sky's the limit.

What's next for you? It's up to you.

Enter your responses to the questions below in your journal.

- What *is* next for you?
- What new possibilities do you see for yourself?
- What obstacles do you see standing between you and those possibilities?
- What are you going to do about it?

THE AWARENESS TRAP

Consider the distinction between awareness and action. Awareness can be a tool to make something happen, or it can be a security blanket to wrap your "issues" up in, to protect and incubate them. Awareness is only one small part of having life work. We all know some amazingly aware people who are also amazingly ineffective. They may be able to analyze, advise, and sermonize, but they prefer to stop there—to cuddle up with their reasons and understanding rather than follow through on that knowledge with action. Awareness is a fairly early phase in the game of having life work. Transformation requires not necessarily that you understand, but that you *change*.

THINGS WILL ALWAYS GET IN YOUR WAY

In the context of "no possibility," which I say is the condition of the drift in which we operate, what happens as soon as you begin to consider committing to something? The little "no possibility" goblins in your mind start sounding the alarm only moments after you have the idea. Then they begin shouting at you. They shout all the reasons why your idea won't work. All at once, they rant at you: "You don't have the time." "You don't have the money." "You failed last time you tried that." "You're too lazy." "Your parents won't let you." "Your husband/wife won't like it." "You don't have the education." "You're too young." "You're too old." "You're too tall, short, fat, thin, pretty, ugly." "A woman can't do that." "A man can't do this." "You never follow through on these ideas." "You don't have enough support." "You don't have the energy." "You're too shy." "The economy isn't right." "It's already been done." "You don't deserve it."

They are so loud that, even if there were an encouraging voice in there somewhere, assuring you that your idea is indeed possible, you wouldn't be able to hear it because of the din created by the screaming goblins.

Who wins? Ninety percent of the time the goblins win. Those pessimistic goblins represent interpretations that extinguish possibilities. They are incredibly powerful conversations that we have culturally and individually. We are so resigned to those "no possibility" conversations that people who voice alternative points of view are dismissed, debated, or even ridiculed as hopeless dreamers. We become "no possibility" goblins for each other ("Are you crazy?" "You need to finish college first." "Where will you get the time?").

Write about your "no possibility" goblins in your journal.

- What are some things you want, but don't have (not necessarily material things)?
- Why don't you have them? What obstacles are in your way?
- Do you ever notice an encouraging voice trying to be heard over the goblins, or is your sense of possibilities completely extinguished?
- Why do you suppose we listen to the 'no possibility' interpretations rather than have a conversation *for* possibility?

The "no possibility" conversation has all of us. What would it take for you to conquer that "no possibility" conversation? If the stakes were high enough, I promise you, you could beat almost any obstacles.

For example, what if someone called you up at the office at 5:00 P.M. promising you $10 million, tax-free, and all you had to do to collect is get yourself to the Mexico City airport by 6:00 A.M. the following morning?

Here come the goblins. In the first place, you only have thirteen hours to handle it. It's after-hours, so your travel agent is gone for the day. You just took a two-week vacation, so you don't have any vacation time left. You are swamped with work to catch up on. You spent all of your extra cash on the vacation and your credit cards are charged to the limit, so you don't have the money to buy a ticket to Mexico City. Explaining to your boss, co-workers, friends, and family that you are going to Mexico City to collect the $10 million you were promised is likely to raise a few eyebrows, to say the least. Maybe it's a con—what if you go through the whole ordeal for nothing? Even if you worked everything out, how are you going to get yourself to Mexico City by 6:00 A.M. the next morning?

The promise was legitimate. There really is $10 million waiting for you in Mexico City. Will you handle getting there? I'll bet you one million of that ten million dollars that you would—spending the time, effort, money, and risking the disapproval of others to do it.

There will always be things that you have to handle on the road to the accomplishment of your goals. That is a fact of life. We make up the part about those things being obstacles. What we call obstacles are simply features of the human condition—part of the package, like your arms and legs. If what you are looking for is a cure to being human, a way to eliminate the struggle of being human, you have been reading the wrong book.

The interpretation that you can be made impotent by things like time, money, approval, education, and energy is an illusion. Your interpretation determines whether those resources run your life for you, or whether you stand for being powerful within the conditions and circumstances life delivers you.

DISCIPLINE

To support your process of being in action, do something every day that will bring consistency and discipline into your practices. Do the same thing, preferably at the same time. It doesn't matter whether it's taking a walk, writing in your journal, having dinner with your family, going to an aerobics class, beginning work at the same time every day, or anything else, so long as it is an activity that contributes to you. Through the discipline demanded by a simple, routine commitment, you will fortify your capacity to commit to and complete projects.

SURRENDER

In the drift, when people think of the word *surrender,* they usually think of giving up, quitting, losing, and being beaten. Surrender, in the sense I am using it, means something different. It means giving yourself over to that which matters to you. It means embracing what life serves you rather than resisting it or comparing it to something else. Surrendering allows you to experience satisfaction while you meet the demands of your commitments.

There are two ways to dedicate yourself to a project: (1) on your terms, or, (2) on the project's terms. The first avenue will inevitably cause frustration and conflict. Remember, the world doesn't care how you feel or what you think, it just keeps "world-ing." You'll do yourself a great favor to accept the world on *its* terms. Choose the games you are committed to, and then surrender to the discipline of those games.

Surrendering allows you peace of mind, if not constant glee. The cost of taking a stand, of living as your commitments, is that a warm, fuzzy feeling will not always be available to you. Do you think that Martin Luther King, Jr., woke up every morning excited out of his mind about what was in front of him that day? What determined his actions, and determines the actions of any committed person, was his dedication to the possibility that his dreams could become reality. When you surrender to your commitments and to the discipline they entail, you experience peace as you move through life, regardless of what specific challenges you are facing day by day.

What difference would surrendering make in your experience? Explore that in your next journal entry.

- Where are you experiencing resistance in your life right now?
- Specifically, what is it that you are resisting?
- What is the payoff for resisting it rather than surrendering to it?
- What would surrendering to it mean? What would you have to do differently?
- What possibilities would surrendering to it open up that your resistance is keeping closed?

VISION

Remind yourself of why you undertook this project in the first place:

- What is your vision for your life?
- What is your vision for the world?
- What are the gifts you bring to the world?
- What would you be like if you were completely authentic, free, passionate?
- What is the experience of life you are looking for?
- Who are the people in your life that matter to you? What new contribution can you make to them?

- What are the commitments in life that matter to you?
- What's next for you?

I end our project with a challenge to you. Friedrich Nietzsche said "Life always gets harder toward the summit—the cold increases, responsibility increases." My challenge to you is this: Climb *always* toward the summit.

ABOUT THE AUTHOR

John Hanley, the president of Lifespring, Inc., has devoted his life to developing nontraditional educational programs for the general public. He founded Lifespring in 1974 and has presided over the program's astonishing growth during the last 15 years. He is a graduate of the University of Wisconsin and a member of the American Society for Training and Development, and has served on the Resource Board of the Young Presidents Organization. He is also an accomplished horseman, with a 400-acre working ranch and a national ranking as a Cutting Horse competitor. Happily married for 24 years, he has three children and lives in Tiburon, California.